W9-DFX-234

Life Injections

Connecting Scripture
To The Human Experience

Richard E. Zajac

CSS Publishing Company, Inc., Lima, Ohio

Copyright © 1998 by
CSS Publishing Company, Inc.
Lima, Ohio

Some scripture quotations are from the *New Revised Standard Version of the Bible,* copyright 1989 by the Division of Christian Education of the National Council of the Churches of Christ in the USA. Used by permission.

Library of Congress Cataloging-in-Publication Data

Zajac, Richard E., 1949-
   Life Injections : connecting Scripture to the human experience / Richard E. Zajac.
      p.   cm.
   ISBN 0-7880-1142-1 (pbk.)
   1. Catholic Church—Sermons. 2. Sermons, American. 3. Zajac, Richard E., 1949- .
I. Title.
BX1756.Z35L54   1998
252'.02—dc21   97-27333
                                                                       CIP

This book is available in the following formats, listed by ISBN:
      0-7880-1142-1   Book
      0-7880-1143-X   IBM 3 1/2
      0-7880-1144-8   MAC
      0-7880-1145-6   Sermon Prep

PRINTED IN U.S.A.

To my mother,
who does more for me
than I deserve.

Table of Contents

Preface

I believe it was Joseph Parker from the City Temple of London who, upon hearing someone describe himself as a self-made man, quipped: "You are a powerful argument against the use of unskilled labor." I'm not by any means a self-made man. I'm a product of the influence of many wonderful people.

I'm indebted to my mother Violet and my late father Edward who implanted within me the values that have shaped my life and my preaching. The Felician Sisters of Assumption School were extraordinary teachers and I'm grateful to have been the beneficiary of their talents. I credit the faculty at the Diocesan Preparatory Seminary for furnishing me with a social conscience and engraving idealism onto my soul. I wish particularly to recognize Carl Puehn whose mark can be found in the structure (introduction-body-conclusion) of the sermons to follow.

I thank as well the parish community of Our Lady of the Blessed Sacrament Church in Depew, New York, and especially Monsignor Joseph Coughlin, who endured my infant years as a homilist and provided the encouragement and the affirmation which saw me through my diaconate into priesthood. I would also like to thank St. Ambrose Church in South Buffalo, New York, where my priestly ministry began. Its pastor, Monsignor William Stanton, had an unbelievable ability to dynamically break open the Gospel and he thus set the standard for preaching which I've struggled to meet. And I wonder where I'd be today if it weren't for the challenge and support which the beautiful people of that parish had given me.

Sisters of Charity Hospital, where I've been the Chaplain for some fourteen years, has been the focal point of my life, and the experiences it has rendered have found their way onto the pages ahead. I would like to thank in particular Sister Margaret Dougherty who has been a joy to work for and Sister Anina Burns of happy memory who often typed my sermons, somehow discerning words from the hen-scratching I provided her. Special thanks to Father Jim Croglio who listens to my sermons before they make the pulpit, and my brother Bob and sister-in-law Ginny and my two nieces Laura and Julie, who often help provide perspective, correction, and challenge. Lastly I thank Lucy Andrus of Parkside Lutheran Church who convinced me to have published what you are about to read.

Introduction

It might have been the sixth grade or maybe the seventh or possibly the eighth. It was the first of May and, as had been the custom at Assumption School, we were required to attend the May Day Rally (to honor the Blessed Virgin Mary) in the parking lot of a nearby foundry. To get there, we proceeded six abreast down the center of the street, meeting other neighborhood schools at various junctions. It was, in essence, a two-mile pilgrimage. Upon arriving at our destination, we were led in a series of prayers by various priests culminating in the benediction of the Blessed Sacrament. Interspersed among the prayers was a sermon usually preached by one of the pastors from the participating schools.

As you would suspect from someone as young as myself, it wasn't something I looked forward to but something I dreaded. It was usually boring and sometimes painfully long. That particular year, I was startled into paying attention when the priest (it was not one of the pastors but a teacher at the local high school) began the sermon with the line: "If a beatnik were passing by here today, he would probably remark: 'Dig those crazy birds!' " I then hung on every word as, agreeing with that "off the wall" remark, he went on to describe species of birds whose habits were similar to those who made it a point to follow the gospel of Christ. The seed for what you are about to read was planted on that day.

I was given the taste of a message that connected God and Scripture to life and I yearned for more. That yearning wasn't to be satisfied until one day, while attending worship at my home parish, I was drawn to an alternate worship service going on in the parish basement. The Newman Center at Buffalo State College was undergoing some renovation and the pastor of the parish I attended offered the basement hall as their temporary home.

Mass had just begun and I took a seat in the back row, a bit intrigued by the somewhat unique setting (at that time) for a liturgy. When it came time for the Sunday sermon, Father Jack Weimer stepped to the lectern and, as he preached, I was taken back to that May Day evening in the parking lot of that foundry. I heard a message that spoke to me and my life in down-to-earth terms, providing the gospel with a relevance which I craved. From that day forward, I regularly worshiped at the Newman Center. Some years later, I would successfully convince Seminary authorities to hire Father Jack Weimer as a professor of homiletics.

That seed planted at the May Day Rally began to take root and grow at the Newman Center, producing a young priest eager to make the pulpit a place where the sermon that was preached would connect the Scripture that was read to a message that could reach steel worker and doctor alike, a message that would speak to the human experience.

My preaching has been graced through the years, thanks to the inspiration of my mentor, Father William G. Stanton, as well as the yearly retreats at the Chautauqua Institution where I was exposed to giants in the field of homiletics such as: John Killinger, the late Doctor Bruce Thielemann (whose illustrative style became mine), Doctor Ernest Campbell (whose lectures at a New York symposium on preaching prompted my collection of images and anecdotes and stories), John Gladstone, William Jackson, Murdo MacDonald, William Sloane Coffin, Walter Burghardt, R. Maurice Boyd, and others.

Thanks to seminars by some of the aforementioned preachers, I became acquainted with the works of Harry Emerson Fosdick, J. Wallace Hamilton, F.W. Boreham, and Halford Luccock. Reading their sermons became a way of unwinding from the numerous night calls that are a regular part of my duties as a hospital chaplain. Many of their thoughts and images and ideas have found their way onto the pages that follow.

Admittedly, what you are about to read could incur criticism for its many illustrations and its too brief a mention of Scripture. But I hold to the fact that they will leave you with something to chew on, something that strikes home when it comes to life, something that is of relevance to both the young and the old, the sick and the well, the rich and the poor.

Each sermon represents over twenty hours of work and, although a majority have been preached over the past few years, there are a few of an older vintage. I hope that you will find the pages that follow inspiring and motivating and able to affect your life in a positive way.

Tears

Scripture Lesson: John 11:3-7, 17, 20-27, 33-45
... Jesus began to weep ...

As a hospital chaplain, I'm well acquainted with tears. Here's an attempt at some perspective.

Several years ago, the advertising industry felt it was important to recognize the talent and the creativity in commercials produced for television. They established the Clio Awards and each year present them for particular commercials of excellence featured during that year.

One of the first winners of a Clio was a commercial hailed by many as the best ever made. It went on to become the standard used by the judges in determining future awards. This award-winning anti-pollution commercial had no speaking parts and no dialogue. The viewer sees a stream running through the middle of a beautiful forest. It isn't long before one begins seeing various types of garbage floating down the stream. At about the same time, a man walks toward the camera. As he gets closer, one recognizes him as a Native American Indian. He stops and looks at all the garbage in the stream. As he stares at the ugliness, the camera zeroes in on his ruddy face and a tear falls from his eye. Although an anti-pollution message flashes across the screen, it isn't necessary. The tear said it all.

I'd like to talk with you today not about Clio Awards or commercials, but about tears. Tears send messages and tears perform functions as nothing else can. Washington Irving wrote that "tears speak more eloquently than ten thousand tongues," and Lord Byron wrote that "you can see farther through a tear than you can through a telescope." Tears are not something we're to be ashamed of but something we are to cherish, because the saddest eyes of all are the eyes that shed no tears.

13

Bear with me now as I attempt to describe the importance of tears. First of all, tears are therapeutic. In 1979, Doctors Walter Scott and Stephen Bloomfield found that people who can cry freely catch fewer colds than people who always hold back their tears. Recent studies have established the fact that there are distinct differences between the chemical content of tears of sorrow and the chemical content of tears of joy. Unlike their counterparts, tears of sorrow contain manganese and prolactin, two drugs that have come to be associated with stress. You can thus truthfully say that crying helps eliminate toxic elements from the body.

A recent study at the University of Pittsburgh has shown that healthy people cry more frequently and feel freer to cry than people who suffer from ulcers or colitis. Since both conditions are closely linked with stress, the sponsor of the study suggests that tears might be a partial solution to relief of those problems. Yet another bit of research found that widows with acquaintances who made it easier for them to cry and express their grief were healthier than widows who experienced less encouragement from others to cry and express their grief.

I could quote research and statistics and studies at length; suffice it to say that there are therapeutic qualities to tears. People who cry easily and readily do a lot better in life than those who don't. "Keep a stiff upper lip" might be good advice in selective situations, but for the most part it can be hazardous to one's health.

So, number one: tears can be therapeutic. Number two: tears send signals of comfort as nothing else can. There is nothing more helpful to a person who is hurting badly than the sight of someone with tears in his or her eyes.

A nurse raised a question once at a conference. She said that she had done something that week that was so unprofessional that it bothered her. A baby she was caring for had died and when the baby's mother came to the nursery she broke into uncontrollable tears as she told her the bad news. She was embarrassed by it and she thought her supervisor was going to feel that she was unprofessional. She wondered if there was anything she could do so that she might not react that same way in the future.

The professor to whom she addressed the question had a great response. He said that in all his work with mothers who have lost children in hospitals or with families who have lost loved ones in ICU's and emergency rooms, the type of reaction which the nurse had when she met the mother was the type of reaction that was most meaningful to the person who suffered the loss. Finding a human being who cared so much that she or he cried supplied them with unbelievable comfort. The professor thus told the nurse that the most professional thing she could have done was what she did — that is, cry with the mother.

Think about it yourself. Who would you like to have with you when you're hurting very badly? Someone who is a stoic? Someone with a stone face? Someone who shows no emotion? Or would you rather have someone who wears the emotions on his or her sleeves, someone whose tear-filled eyes telegraph the news that he or she cares about you and your pain? If someone you love had died and someone had to break the bad news, would you prefer a professional rattling off the facts or would you prefer a human being who is not afraid to let the emotions do some of the talking?

Number one: tears can be therapeutic. Number two: tears send signals of comfort as nothing else can. Number three: tears bond us to others in ways seldom experienced.

Khalil Gibran writes that we can easily forget those with whom we've laughed but we can never forget those with whom we've cried.

I read recently of a man whose partner at work had grown seriously ill and was given but a short time to live. The man visited the partner on a regular basis and each time he did so, he fought off the tears as he caught his partner up on the goings-on at work. Finally on one of his visits, he decided to bare his soul; he decided not to fight off the tears. When he did so, his partner felt free to do the same. Writing about that visit, the man said that it was a moment in his life that he'll never forget. "It might sound funny to say this," he wrote, "but we formed a bond when we shared our tears that even his death will not sever."

That is one of the missing elements in society today. People may have many relationships, but in none of them do they feel safe enough to express their hurts, their pains, their tears. So when they finally come upon a relationship in which they can share those pains and those tears, it is something special indeed. A bond develops that knows no equal.

Number one: tears can be therapeutic. Number two: tears can send signals of comfort as nothing else can. Number three: tears bond us to others in ways seldom experienced. Number four: tears can provide valuable insights into the real meaning of life.

A traveler lost in the desert despaired of ever finding water. He struggled up one hilltop, then another, in the hope of sighting a stream. He kept looking in every direction with no success. As he staggered onward, his foot caught on a dry bush and he stumbled to the ground. That is where he lay, with no energy to rise, no desire to struggle anymore, no hope of surviving the ordeal. As he lay there, helpless and dejected and full of tears, he suddenly became aware of the silence of the desert. On all sides a majestic stillness reigned, undisturbed by the slightest sound. Suddenly he raised his head. He heard something, something so faint that only the sharpest ear and the desert silence could lead to its detection: it was the sound of running water. Heartened by the hope that the sound aroused in him, he rose and kept moving until he arrived at the stream of fresh, cool water.

Our tears have a way of alerting us to the streams of life-giving waters. When we are filled with the deepest of emotions, it is often because we've lost something that we loved dearly. And that loss awakens us to the valuable things of life that, heretofore, we overlooked and reminds us how trivial are the things that usually occupy our attention. Knocked to the ground by the sorrow we've experienced, we tend to be in a much better position to hear and to find the streams of life-giving waters where real happiness happens to be, where the true meaning of life can be discovered, streams that eluded us before our tears were shed.

I'm reminded of Robert Browning's poem:

I walked a mile with pleasure,
She chattered all the way.
But left me none the wiser,
for all she had to say.

16

I walked a mile with sorrow
and ne'er a word said she,
But Oh! the things I learned from her
when sorrow walked with me.

Tears can be therapeutic. Tears send signals of comfort as nothing else can. Tears bond us to others in ways seldom experienced. Tears can provide valuable insights into the real meaning of life. And tears are a sign of courage and strength.

I remember when I was growing up, after I got past the age of seven, if my parents caught me crying about something, they would tell me to stop or otherwise I would really have something to cry about. I, along with many others, was taught at an early age that crying was for babies, that crying is inappropriate behavior for big kids. So, as we grew up, it was expected that we keep a stiff upper lip, that we show courage by holding back our tears. Now that might be fine for the petty affairs of life, but when it comes to honest grief, real courage lies in the shedding of tears. It is the courage to face straightforwardly the pain and sorrow of a loss, to deal with it and not suppress it with a phony facade of strength.

I think you all remember that beautiful real-life story of Brian Piccolo and Gale Sayers, two big, strong football players for the Chicago Bears. Their story was captured in a television movie called *Brian's Song*. They were the first black man and white man to room together in professional football. Tragedy struck as Brian Piccolo contracted cancer, a disease he was destined not to beat despite all the effort in the world.

As Piccolo neared death, Gale Sayers went on alone to an awards banquet where he was to receive the George Halas Award for being the most courageous football player in the NFL. As Sayers approached the microphone just after he was presented the award, tears ran unashamedly down his face. He proclaimed how he loved Brian Piccolo and how sick Brian was, and that Brian deserved the award more than he. He said: "When you hit your knees tonight, please ask God to love Brian Piccolo." As he concluded his talk with those words, the viewer cried right along with him. Gale Sayers was most certainly a man of undeniable strength and courage, and his outward shedding of tears did much to dispel the myth that crying is a sign of weakness.

One of the biggest things I learned in my training for chaplaincy was that it is all right for me to cry in my ministry with people who are hurting very deeply. It took more courage for me to risk showing emotion than it did for me to hold it back. I learned that when I show my tears, I am a stronger chaplain.

Tears can be therapeutic. Tears send signals of comfort as nothing else can. Tears bond us to others in ways seldom experienced. Tears can provide valuable insights into the real meaning of life. Tears are a sign of courage and strength. And, lastly, tears can be a means of prayer.

A reporter was once interviewing an Indian guru about his work in giving spiritual instructions to Americans. The reporter asked the spiritual master: "What is the first spiritual thing you attempt to teach Americans?" The old man replied: "I try to teach them how to cry again."

It is so often true that when tears flow, it usually means we are in a situation that touches us very deeply, one that reaches down to the roots of our humanity, one that helps us to realize it is God who is in charge and not us. When tears flow, it is a deeply spiritual event. We are more in touch with God at that time than we are when we are down on our knees.

I know of a family with three children, two girls and a boy. The boy went off to summer camp for the first time. A week later, the rest of the family drove to meet him. They had a great visit, but the time came to say good-bye. The wee fellow was homesick. The sisters missed their brother. As they drove away in their car, one of the girls said through her tears: "I know what to do. Let's pray for him." And the other little girl replied: "I can't pray for him. I'm too busy crying." The truth of the matter, of course, was that she was praying for him. Every tear, you see, was a prayer. God hears the prayers that flow from our hearts and tears lay a stronger claim onto our hearts than any words we can possibly compose.

I have spent all this time extolling the benefits of tears because I believe that tears are befitting a follower of Christ. Today's Gospel happens to contain the shortest verse in all of scripture, the verse "Jesus wept." And he wept not just for Lazarus but for all of us, showing us that crying need not be something to be ashamed of or something to avoid. By crying himself, our Lord showed us that crying is not something reserved for babies or sissies, but it is something hallowed by God.

So when tears well up in your eyes, do not be so quick to hold them back. Try letting them run freely. You might be ridding your body of toxic wastes. You might be sending needed signals of comfort to someone who is hurting. You might be bonding yourself to someone in a way you have always longed for but never experienced. You might be putting yourself in a position where you will finally hear and find the streams of water where real happiness and fulfillment happen to be. You might be courageously showing how much you care. Or you may even be in the midst of prayer.

Bear with me for one final story. It is an old Rabbinic tale about Moses and the chosen people. The citizens of heaven are watching them as they cross the Red Sea. When they reach the other side, Moses raises his staff and the Egyptian army and their horses and chariots get swept into the sea to their deaths. A great cheer breaks out among the citizens of heaven. Everyone is full of joy. As they start high-fiving each other, they notice that God is not joyful. As a matter of fact, God is crying huge tears. An angel says: "God, what's the matter? Your chosen people are safe. They're victorious." God, wiping away the tears from his cheeks, says to the angel: "Yes, I know, but you see, the Egyptians are my people too." ... Jesus wept; God wept. So can we.

The Golden Years

Scripture Lesson: Luke 2:22-40

... There was also a prophet, Anna ... she was of a great age ...

The Feast of the Presentation is periodically celebrated on a Sunday, thrusting Simeon and Anna, two of the most famous of scriptural senior citizens, onto the Gospel stage. This is a good time to reflect on themes relating to the elderly.

In my opinion the most creative things on television today are the commercials. They always seem much more imaginative and far more ingenious than are the sitcoms, the soap operas, and the dramas that populate the airwaves. There's an interesting one for Budweiser beer that has caught my attention, especially in the way it turns the tables on our expectations.

It begins with a group of young men enjoying a game of hockey on a frozen body of water. Then elderly men with axes in their hands head right toward them. For a minute, you think you're watching a promo for a Stephen King movie. You figure they're going to attack with those axes, when all of a sudden they start chopping up the ice. The next minute they're diving in and out of the frozen water having a whale of a time, looking like a bunch of kids around a swimming hole on a summer day. It ends with their enjoying a beer with the young hockey players who can't believe those old buzzards could do what they happened to be doing.

I begin with that commercial not to promote Budweiser beer, but to touch upon something that the commercial brings to light: our attitudes, our assumptions, our expectations when it comes to the elderly. As we have a habit of doing with ethnic groups and with particular races of people, we hold up stereotypical images of old people and we seldom take note of how far from the truth those stereotypical images are.

Since two senior citizens, Simeon and Anna, are on the center stage of our Gospel, I thought I'd spend some time today talking about old age, beginning with a review of the commonly held stereotypes which, upon closer examination, are a far cry from the way things really are. First and foremost, most would say that with old age comes a decline in memory.

It's always interesting that when someone twenty years of age forgets where he put his glasses, no one makes a comment. But when a senior citizen does the same, it's automatically assumed that the memory is starting to go; it's automatically assumed that senility is just a heartbeat away. Now it is true that people in their seventies experience some drop-off in the ability to remember certain events, but other types of memory — for knowledge, for facts, for skill — they're not affected at all. Aptitude and intelligence tests have revealed very little drop-off in mental ability as the ages pile on. Senior citizens are just as capable of learning as are younger people. Contrary to popular opinion, old dogs can learn new tricks. And when it comes to senility, we're talking about a physical disease that strikes only a small portion of the elderly. It is not a foregone conclusion of old age.

Then there's the stereotype that has senior citizens cast as inflexible and set in their ways. You can probably bet that if there's an old person who fits that description, it's because he's been inflexible and set in his ways all his life. Ben Franklin once wrote that some people die at 25 and aren't buried until they're 75. Negative character traits are usually born in childhood and nurtured along until old age.

I remember when all the changes were going on back in the days of the Vatican Council, one of the knocks on the church was that it was chasing away all the old people. All the changes were causing dismay for the senior citizens. But as things went, the elderly were usually the most receptive to change. It was actually the middle-aged who had the biggest problem accepting the differences within the church. They were far more inflexible than any of their elder brothers or sisters.

Following along the list of stereotypes is that productivity drops off with the coming of age. There are just too many examples refuting that argument. Think of Moses, who at the age of eighty led three million people out of captivity; or Thomas Edison who at 85 invented the mimeograph machine; or Pablo Casals who was still giving solo concerts at 88. At the same age, the famous Michelangelo enjoyed drafting excellent architectural plans for great cathedrals that stand yet today as monuments not only to his eternal God but also to the accomplishments of an aging giant. Tennyson was 83 when he penned his immortal poem *Crossing the Bar.* At 100 years of age Grandma Moses was still painting; at 92, George Bernard Shaw was still writing plays; at 89, Albert Schweitzer headed a hospital in Africa. The list is endless: John XXIII, Mother Teresa, George Burns. Creative and inventive contributions continue to be made by people well into the golden years. Productivity doesn't drop off just because people are old.

Whatever the stereotype might be that's attached to old age, the facts and truths are there to refute that claim.

I'm raising issues on aging today because the Feast of the Presentation highlights two of the most famous biblical senior citizens, Simeon and Anna. By becoming the vehicle of the Lord's consecration to his Father, their stature and their dignity are raised a hundredfold. I believe it was planned that way by God to underline the fact that being old is not something lamentable but something praiseworthy, that the elderly are not appendages to society but an integral part of society, that old men or old women are not to be labeled and discarded as useless, but should be honored and embraced and held up as privileged members of God's kingdom. So we are called on this Feast of the Presentation to examine our attitudes toward the elderly and to put aside the assumptions and stereotypes that have ways of demeaning and degrading their worth and dignity.

The Polish have an expression that is often on the lips of those in their community who are getting up in age and who are starting to feel their age. The expression is "Starosc nie radosc," which loosely translated means "it is no fun to get old." It is unfortunately the sentiment shared by Pole and non-Pole alike.

Besides his telling us to hold senior citizens in high esteem, God is also telling the seniors to hold themselves in high esteem. For far too many, that's a growing problem. Besides the negative attitudes and assumptions toward the elderly, there's also the matter of negative attitudes and assumptions toward aging itself. "Starosc nie radosc" is echoed loudly and often as far too many see the advent of the golden years as a curse instead of a blessing.

There is an old story about two girls who went for a walk in the country together. When they got back home, they were asked how things went. One talked about nothing but the dusty roads and the flies and the heat and the general discomforts. The other talked about a clump of bluebells growing out of a rock and the glimpse of the sea at the turn in the road and the sight of the cardinal on one of the branches of a tree. She reported it with a gleam in her eye. It reminds me of the old couplet: "Two men looked out the prison bars, one saw mud, the other saw stars."

The matter of whether aging is a blessing or a curse depends on how we view it. Surely there are a lot of negatives to aging, but there are also a lot of positives. You can look at the grey hairs, the growing aches and pains, the decrease in vision or in hearing; or you can look at the wisdom that's now had, the insights into life that are so much broader, the opportunities to do things that were never there before. There are dust and flies and mud when it comes to aging, but there are also bluebells and cardinals and stars.

When I went over the list of octogenarians who achieved greatness, I neglected to point out that many excelled, not in their first careers, but in their second careers. With the raising of a family behind them, with a general lessening of commitments and responsibilities, they had the time to pursue jobs, hobbies, and activities that they wouldn't have thought of pursuing when they were young.

Henry Wadsworth Longfellow was asked on his eightieth birthday how it was that he was having such a good time being old. In response, he pointed to a cherry tree in blossom, asking in turn where the blossoms were. The answer was "on the new wood." The tree kept its life by growing new life. It's the new branches that have added to the blossoms of the tree. Longfellow made aging fun by using the extra time aging gave him to pursue new adventures, to grow new branches on his tree.

I'm reminded of an elderly woman who was rescued from the brink of despair by her doctor. He suggested that she learn to paint. She took him up on his suggestion and, in due time, she found a new interest, new friends, and a whole world she had not known before in museums and art galleries. New blossoms came because she grew new wood.

The golden years provide its bearers with the extra time that can be cashed in for the new pursuits, the new adventures, and the new directions that could never be pursued in the responsibility-filled younger years of life.

With old age comes the ability to know the difference between what is important and what is not, what is to be hallowed and what is to be cast aside, what is to be remembered and what is to be forgotten. I like what Rabbi Sidney Greenberg wrote in his book *How to Say Yes to Life.*[1] He calls time the "thoughtful thief" because for everything it steals from us, it gives us something in return. He says," While time was stealing the smoothness of our skins, it was giving us the opportunity to remove the wrinkles from our souls." There comes with the onset of age the realization that life is too short to be petty and evil and cruel. Age helps unveil that which is harmful to the soul.

There are growing limitations that are part and parcel of the senior years. Even at the tender age of 42, I can't do all the things I used to do, and it's a frightening thought to realize that there may come a time when I may have to ask people to come to my assistance. No one likes to relinquish independence, but sometimes, with the coming of age, there isn't a choice. What you have to realize is that by reaching out for help, you're performing a valuable service for another human being. You're giving a younger man or woman a chance to be unselfish.

An American traveled to India to visit an old friend who was doing missionary work. While the two of them were walking through the streets of Calcutta, a beggar approached the visitor and asked for alms. Instinctively, the American reached into his pocket and placed some change in the old man's hand, at which point the missionary instructed his American friend to say, "Thank you." A few minutes later, after the old man had gone, the American asked his missionary friend why he was the one to say thank you instead of the beggar. In a voice that indicated that he expected the question, the missionary gently answered: "In this country, we believe that the poor give us the opportunity to perform a good deed for which there is far greater reward, and so we thank them for the chance to put our faith into practice."

If age makes us dependent on others, just think of the blessings we're bestowing on others.

With onset of old age, we can bemoan its limitations or we can see in the aging process immense opportunity for joy, happiness, peace, and service. It comes down to whether we see bluebirds or dust, the mud or the stars. Aging can be a blessing or a curse; the choice is ours.

This Feast of the Presentation, this feast of Simeon and Anna, is God's way of raising our consciousness not only as to the worth and value of senior citizens, but also to the worth and value of the aging process itself. So put the stereotypes to rest. See the blessing side of old age. Celebrate the beauty and the wonder that surround the Simeons and Annas of our time. And if you see a group of senior citizens jumping in and out of an ice-filled pond, chalk it up as a sign of the vigor and vitality of old age.

———————

1. Sidney Greenberg, *Say Yes to Life* (New York: Cross Books, 1982), p. 63.

Make Good Use Of Your Injustice

Scripture Lesson: Philippians 2:1-11
... he emptied himself taking the form of a slave ...

As awful and as undeserving as adversity can be, it can often work a blessing.

Recently I was called to the ICU to minister to a patient about to undergo surgery. When I arrived in the unit, I came to discover that the gentleman I was to see was rapidly failing. He had an aneurysm that was bleeding, and even with the surgery, his chances for survival were slim. I blessed and anointed the man and then went out to find the family. They were all, as you would imagine, quite devastated. And what made this particular situation even more distressing was the fact that the day before they had all attended a funeral. The daughter of the man having the surgery had taken her life. He had been at the funeral along with his entire family. Here was this group of people in the waiting room, reeling from the grief of losing a daughter and sister, and now in the throes of even more tragedy. Four hours later, their worst fears were realized. The surgery was unsuccessful. The patient died. It was for me another example of the uncertainty of the human experience. They didn't deserve to have one tragedy thrust upon them, to say nothing of a double disaster.

Too many people live with the illusion that we get what we have coming to us, that life is structured in such a way that one can expect justice to be served. Despite the accumulated experiences of the ages, too many people hold to the myth that for every good deed we do, life will pay us a corresponding amount of happiness; that for every positive action performed, a just reward will instantaneously follow. Now admittedly, that is partially true. Good deeds, good actions, carry with them satisfaction and fulfillment. But to suggest that they grant one an immunity from trouble, to suggest that they shield one from life's adversities, to suggest that such goodness exempts one from the horrors of life! All these presumptions fall short of the truth. Bad things happen, period. They don't seek out the most deserving; they simply occur without regard for the lifestyle or the life story of their victims.

I raise this point today because it is important for people to understand that, but also because the injustices of life, as bad as they might be, can sometimes bring about a blessing. The unfairness built into life can sometimes stimulate passions and strengths never known before. So many of the heroes and giants of our time became that way precisely because of life's injustices. As awful and as undeserving as adversity can be, it can flush out of people tremendous virtue. It can put them in touch with a depth of understanding and a quality of courage not present when life follows an easier path.

The Jewish activist Natan Sharansky was imprisoned by the Soviet government on false charges of spying. He was sentenced to fifteen years of hard labor. He could have spent his days in deep dejection and utter despair, but he accepted his unfair fate and utilized the experience to fuel his resolve and to strengthen his determination and purpose. He left the prison a much stronger man than when he entered. His ability to make positive use of his adversity has not only won him worldwide acclaim, but it has made him an inspiration to all those unjustly bound. One can say much the same for Nelson Mandela. He, too, used his injustice well. He, too, emerged from prison as a giant to all his countrymen struggling with the unfairness of apartheid.

Harry Emerson Fosdick told of a friend who was visiting the state of Maine. He came upon an apple tree so loaded with fruit that the laden branches were propped to keep them from the ground. When the friend inquired about it, the owner of the orchard said, "Go look at that tree's trunk near the bottom." This friend went and examined it and discovered that the tree had been badly wounded with a deep gash. "That's something we learned about apple trees," said the owner of the orchard. "When the trees tend to run to wood and leaves and not to fruit, we wound it and gash it, and almost always, no one knows why, this is the result: it turns its energies into fruit."

That is one of the marvelous things about life's injustices. They have often resulted in the production of multiple fruits in the lives of many people. As we have seen with the lives of Sharansky and Mandela, there's something about the wounds and gashes of life's terrible trials that can bring out of people virtues and qualities they never knew before.

Booker T. Washington once coined the phrase "the advantage of disadvantage." Born a black slave, allowed to carry the books of his white master's children to the schoolhouse door but never to enter it himself, he was shut out from the area of privilege he craved most. The advantage of his disadvantage was far from obvious. Yet out of that early slavery, with its cruel injustices, he won an appreciation for education and a determination to get it for himself at any cost. This injustice led to his passion to open doors for all black youth, a passion that could never have had such depth and poignancy had it not been spurred by his own privations. Booker T. Washington became the great giant he was not *despite* his experiences of injustice but in a large measure *because* of them.

It is important that we not only realize that life is not fair or just, but that should we be victims of injustice we take out of the experience the lessons it can teach us. We should come out of the experience better, wiser, deeper persons. Even if that injustice leaves us wounded and crippled, it will have opened to us insight, understanding, and empathy which we never had before.

Two missionaries lost their only daughter to leprosy. "This is the outcome of our service to India." They could have said that with bitterness and anger. They could have railed forever at the injustice of it all. But instead, they came back to India determined to do something for lepers who were suffering as their daughter had suffered. They established the Purulia Leper Asylum, which has grown into one of the largest and best leper colonies in the world. This tragic loss of their only daughter would open for two missionaries the reality of a need they would never have seen had it not touched them directly. Insight, understanding, and empathy take on a new depth whenever an injustice strikes a life. Needs are seen more clearly; hurts are sensed more deeply; concerns and sympathy are registered more convincingly.

A friend told me his experience with open-heart surgery. He said many people came to talk to him about the surgery but he hardly listened. The one exception came when someone arrived who had gone through the surgery himself. Suddenly, he said, his ears perked up; he hung on every word the person said. Here was one who walked the same path he was to walk. Here was someone who knew firsthand precisely what he would be going through. That someone had an integrity only gained by the fact that he had borne the pains and fears of open-heart surgery.

Those who have been burned by injustice have that same kind of status. They can reach out to fellow victims as no one else can. They have a sensitivity that escapes those who can only read about or hear about the injustice that might be unfolding. Their wounds provide a credibility, an authority, and a power as nothing else can.

One of the most influential reformers of England's humanitarian movement of the nineteenth century which abolished debtor prison, improved conditions of labor, and cleansed the English schools of their worst disciplinary barbarities was Charles Dickens. He was not simply a marvelous storyteller; he was an effective reformer. In his writings, he vividly described the abominations of his time. But what made them so real and effective was that he had suffered from those same abominations. Micawber, Dicken's father, had been in a debtors' prison. As a young boy, crushed with shame and crippled with poverty, Dickens had gone up to the depressing prison day after day to visit him. When ten years old, he worked long hours for a pittance pasting labels on bottles in a blacking factory. Dickens endured the stupid cruelties of an old school system. His exposé on all those social ills of his time took on a power and strength because they were written by a man who had been there, who had walked the same valley of darkness as the people about whom he wrote.

That brings me at last to the inspiration for my remarks. It was today's Second Reading. Saint Paul tells the Philippians how Christ emptied himself; how he took the form of a slave; how he accepted and handled death on the cross — a death that had injustice written all over it. We believe the Lord chose the human experience deliberately. This was a signal to us that even he wasn't exempt from the unfairness of life. It was his wish to let us know that should we be victimized by injustice we have an ally in him. We can find his concern and his love credible because he knows firsthand all that we are going through. The family I mentioned earlier who underwent two tragedies, I'm sure, felt God's presence very deeply. He was surely their ally. He knew what they were going through.

An old saying declares: "When fate throws a dagger at you, there are two ways to catch it: either by the blade or by the handle. Catch the dagger by the blade and it may cut you, perhaps kill you. But if you catch it by the handle, you can use it to fight your way through whatever it is that you are dealing with." When life throws a dagger of injustice at you, realize first that God is with you. Then grab it by the handle and ask God to help you use the awful experience to broaden and deepen your life, to bring out the Sharansky or the Mandela or the Washington or the Dickens that might be living within you. When life throws a dagger of injustice at you, grab it by the handle and use your newfound kinship with those who are hurting to propel you to seek reforms or address needs that you are now in a much better position to understand.

I wish I could tell you that life is fair and just, but it isn't. If you have realized that already, thank God. But if the dagger should come your way, grab it by the handle and not by the blade.

Bad Habits

Scripture Lesson: Mark 9:38-43, 47-48
  ... if your eye causes you to stumble, tear it out ...

A formula for adherence to some rather grizzly instructions.

I read recently of a man who went to see his doctor. After the checkup, the doctor told him, "The best thing you can do is stop drinking, go on a diet, start jogging, and stop carousing around town to all hours of the night." The man stood there, stroked his beard, thought for a moment. Then he said to the doctor: "What's the next best thing?"

I chuckled when I read it and I'm sorry to say it, but I can almost see myself responding in the same way — not that my lifestyle matches his, not that the doctor would provide the same advice for me — but because it's very, very hard to end old habits and begin new ones.

Charles Dickens, in *A Tale of Two Cities,*[1] provides one of the most tragic examples of that reality. A man was held captive for many long years in the dreaded prison known as the Bastille. He lived in a dark cell where his daily job was the monotonous hammering of shoes. When he was finally released, when he was finally liberated, he witnessed for the first time in years the beautiful sky, the sunshine, the sound of birds singing, and air blowing through the trees. When he arrived at his English home, the first thing he did was to build a room that had the exact dimensions of that prison cell that he lived in for those many long years. People who came to visit would always find him sitting in the dark, hammering away at shoes.

Now lest we think that's something out of the imagination of a Charles Dickens, consider, if you will, friends of yours who have finally forsaken the habit of smoking or who finally quit drinking. One might think that a morning free of coughing or a morning devoid of a hangover would be a welcome and liberating change, but how often has it happened that those very friends soon went back to those old habits? The reality is that it is very, very hard to end old habits and begin new ones even when those old habits have all the earmarks of a Bastille prison.

I raise the issue of habits today because that was the focus of Jesus' strong remarks at the conclusion of today's Gospel. When he talked about cutting off a hand or foot or plucking out an eye, Jesus wasn't speaking literally. He was speaking about jettisoning from our life that which has become so deeply ingrained within us that it has actually become a part of us. Habits have that nature.

C.S. Lewis tells of a woman who complained habitually. Finally it was no longer possible to describe her accurately by saying she had a complaint. The truth is that she had become a complaint. It was impossible to separate her from her complaining. People do the same thing with self-pity, serenading others with several versions of "woe is me." There are those who are always despairing, always cynical, always providing a gloomy outlook on life. We know how they will answer any question we ask or how they'll react to things. Their habits have made them predictable. Their complaining, their cynicism, their gloom have become as much a part of them as their hand or their foot or their eye. And the saddest thing of all is that for the most part, they're not even aware that is so.

I'm reminded of that cartoonist who was asked to draw caricatures, those drawings in which people's habits and idiosyncracies are highlighted. He passed the sketches around for everyone to look at. There were plenty of laughs. But the funny thing was that everyone recognized everyone else, but none of them recognized themselves.

That's the insidious nature of habits. They slowly creep into people's lives. People will do something once, they'll behave in a certain way once. Then they do it again the second time and, before long, they do it all the time. It becomes second nature; it becomes so much a part of their routine that they become oblivious to the fact that they're doing it.

That's all fine and good when we're talking about something positive but it's not so fine and good when we're talking about something negative. In those cases, damage is inflicted unbeknown to the host; in those cases, the bad habit doesn't reach the level of awareness until it's almost too late.

A colleague was telling me about a parishioner, a bank official who was charged with stealing thousands of dollars from a bank where he had worked for more than twenty years. Before his arrest he was one of the most beloved workers in the bank and one of the most respected men in the community. One day after closing hours, he innocently and accidentally took some money home. Realizing his mistake and realizing that he couldn't take it back that night, he set it aside, fully intending to return it the next morning. As it turned out, he forgot, so he had to juggle the books to cover his oversight. He still intended to return the money.

When he headed out the door of his home the next morning, he grabbed the money, but then he thought about it for a while. By juggling the books, he knew the bank wouldn't miss it. Then he told himself that he was really underpaid and he needed the money more than the bank did, so he kept it. Soon it happened again, and he rationalized keeping it again. He did this for over two years before finally getting caught.

When my colleague sat down and talked with him, the bank official said that he couldn't believe what a thief he had become. He had so deluded himself with rationalizations — he was so blind to his own bad habits — that he couldn't see what was happening. He was unaware of what he had become.

The first step in cutting off the foot and the hand of a bad habit, the first step in gouging out the eye of bad behavior is honestly to recognize it; to take notice of how slowly it has crept into the fabric of our life; to see how we've become synonymous with complaining or self-pity or cynicism; to see how we've become a thief, an alcoholic, an adulterer, a gossip, or an egotist; to see how we've become surly or selfish or rude. Once we've accepted that and owned up to that, the next step is to try to stop it.

When Ben Franklin found himself beset with bad habits, he concocted a strategy to overcome them. He made a list of thirteen virtuous goals such as temperance, moderation, order, and so forth. He then constructed a little calendar book with rows of the virtues and columns of the days of the week. He focused on one virtue each week and at the end of each day would put a black mark on his chart if he had violated the virtue that day. In this way, Franklin gradually gained good habits and that helped to minimize his bad ones.

That strategy might not work in the case of our bad habits, but its basic premise makes sense. If once we've accepted and recognized how a bad behavior or a negative practice has nailed down a corner of our life, the way to stop it, the way to overcome it, is to substitute a positive habit and to do so one day at a time.

I'm reminded of a Max Beerbohm story[2] which featured a debauched and unvirtuous man named Lord George Hell who fell in love with an innocent and saintly young woman. In order to woo and win her, he covered his shifty features with the mask of a saint. Years later a wicked lady from George Hell's past came to town and sought to expose him for the scoundrel and fake she knew him to be. Confronting him in front of his wife, she dared him to take off his mask. Sadly, he took it off and to their great amazement discovered that beneath the mask of a saint was now the face of a saint. By playing the part, by taking on the habits of a saint, Lord George Hell managed to put to rest the less than saintly habits that had previously colored his life.

We might be tempted to write that story off as a piece of fiction, as something out of a make-believe world, but it does speak to a truth. It provides the strategy for overcoming bad habits.

Raul Julia, whom you might know as the actor who portrayed the lead character in the Addams Family movies, was someone whose real life left much to be desired. He had fallen away from the church. He had acquired more than his share of bad habits. One day he was recruited and signed to play the part of Archbishop Oscar Romero in a movie. Taking on the habits and daily activities of the Archbishop, acting out the role of a man whom many consider both a martyr and a saint, Raul Julia found himself becoming moved and enriched by what he was doing. In striking similarity to his fictional counterpart Lord George Hell, Julia, in playing the part of a saint, became a changed man. He returned to church, became involved in many worthwhile activities, and slowly began to shed his bad habits.

Don't get me wrong! I'm not suggesting that we all go out and pretend that we're saints — no one likes a phony — but I am suggesting that we start doing positive things, that we start acting in virtuous ways, that we begin taking on good habits. If we do that consistently, one day at a time, there's no telling its ability to transform us in much the same way it transformed Lord George Hell, Raul Julia, and Ben Franklin.

If we are to heed Christ's Gospel command, if we are to jettison the bad habits that have become as much a part of us as our hands or feet or eyes, we must recognize that reality: how we've grown synonymous with complaining or self-pity or cynicism; how we've deluded ourselves with rationalizations that neatly excuse our alcoholism, our selfishness, our callousness, our rudeness. Second, we must put on the mask of a saint, we must act the part of good habits. Like Ben Franklin, we must make it a point to demonstrate on a daily basis some virtue that will begin to overcome a vice. And lastly, we must make sure that we move in circles where those tasks will be supported.

One of the biggest frustrations of drug counselors, of social workers assigned to furloughed prisoners, of psychologists dealing with people with self-destructive habits is the fact that their clients either live in or go back to an environment that not only helped breed the bad habits but which also does not support their efforts to change. Study after study has confirmed that when you run with winners you become a winner; when you run with losers you become a loser. You can't expect to shed a bad habit if you run with losers. You have to find yourself some winners, some people, a group who will encourage you in your efforts to change, who will support you in your attempts to jettison the habit that is destroying you.

It is very, very hard to end old habits and begin new ones. As the cobbler in the Bastille prison demonstrated, all too often we prefer those old habits no matter how destructive or how limiting or how oppressive they may be. There's not a person among us who does not have some old bad habit that needs to be cut out and gouged out. May we heed Christ's Gospel command and take action starting today.

1. Described by Harry E. Fosdick, *The Three Meanings* (New York: Garden City Books, 1951), p. 196.

2. Described by Frederick Buechner, *Telling the Truth* (New York: Harper & Row, 1977), p. 80.

Top Ten List

Scripture Lesson: Matthew 18:21-25
*... if another member of the church sins against me,
how often should I forgive ...*

David Letterman helped inspire this talk on forgiveness.

What I like about David Letterman and his late-night talk show is not just his offbeat humor, but also some of the bits that have become a regular part of the show. One of those bits is the top ten list. It has become a signature item for Letterman. He uses it to poke fun at some topic that might have surfaced in the news during a particular week.

Today's Gospel is about forgiveness. Although Letterman uses the top ten list to poke fun and elicit laughter, here is a serious version concentrating on the topic of forgiveness. Here are the top ten reasons why we need to practice forgiveness.

Reason Number 10 is because the failure to do so can have epic repercussions.

Recently the Parliament of World Religions met in Chicago. The entire week was an effort to forge some common ground among the ten world religions. It was an effort to secure people in their own religion while at the same time looking for ways we might work together on common problems.

One of the plenary sessions was: "The Voices of the Dispossessed." People representing areas of the world where human rights have been violated, where injustice, persecution, and terrorism were rampant, were invited to speak. Things went smoothly until someone from Kashmir spoke. Suddenly shouts were heard from the audience. The same thing happened when a Sikh spoke of the persecution of his people. Tension filled the air, for there were various groups in the audience who had different perspectives on the Sikh and Kashmir problem.

The disputing parties, that unfortunately are drawn along religious lines, have been at each other's throats for hundreds of years. The whole thing started when one family wronged another family, and no effort toward forgiveness and reconciliation was ever made. Things started to escalate, and centuries later the acrimony, the hatred, and the thirst for vengeance have reached epic proportions involving hundreds of thousands of people.

Dominique Henri Pire, the winner of the 1958 Nobel Prize, once said, "If an atomic bomb falls on the world tomorrow, it is because I argued with my neighbor today." The failure to forgive can have tragic and epic consequences because there is no telling the escalation of the bad blood and the bad spirit between you and the person who wronged you.

Reason Number 9 as to why we need to practice forgiveness is that the failure to do so can have a poisonous effect on our personalities and our character.

According to the folklore of the Pima Indians, we are all born having a stone with spikes sticking out of it positioned right next to our heart. If a person hurt or neglected someone or did something to break down a relationship, the stone would begin to turn, and it continued to turn until the situation was set aright or corrected. According to this fascinating legend, although the spikes rubbed against the heart, they did not cut or puncture it. They merely rubbed and rubbed until the heart became more and more calloused. In that way, the longer one waited to correct a situation, the longer one waited to practice forgiveness and reconciliation, the more calloused became one's heart. Although it is all a matter of folklore, nothing comes closer to the truth. The failure to practice forgiveness can espouse bitterness and resentment, and that can only serve to harden one's heart and in the process poison one's personality and character.

Reason Number 8 is because the person who wronged us may not know that he or she did so.

In Anthony Robbins' latest book[1] he makes a point about rules: all of us operate out of different sets of rules. The basis of every emotional upset we've ever had with another human being is in reality a rules upset. Somebody did something or failed to do

40

something that violated one of our rules about what he or she must or should do.

For example, some people's rule for respect is: "If you respect me, then you never raise your voice." So if a person with whom you're in a relationship suddenly starts to yell, you're not going to feel respected if that's your rule. You're going to feel angry because it has been violated. Other people, on the other hand, may be living by a different set of rules. They may be living by the rule that being respectful means being truthful about all their feelings and all their emotions — good, bad, or indifferent — and they express them with all their intensity. With that kind of scenario, one person can hurt another person and not feel that he or she did so at all.

If forgiveness is practiced, that sort of rule conflict is brought to light. If forgiveness is practiced, the air is cleared about differences in philosophy, and greater sensitivity can be practiced by all concerned.

Reason Number 7 is that the person who hurt you may have done so because he or she has been hurt.

We've been hearing a lot these days of the stain that's left in people when their childhood has been brutalized by abuse or neglect. Chances are that later in life that very stain will exemplify itself in similar behavior. That's not excusing the perpetrator of a hurt; that's not suggesting that we let things go without saying anything about it. It's just that we need to realize that people sometimes do bad things because they've been hurt deeply by someone who did bad things to them. The practice of forgiveness can bring that to light.

Reason Number 6 as to why we should practice forgiveness is that the person who hurt us may have been trying to help us.

Anaximenes, the old cynic philosopher, used to say that there are only two people who can tell us the truth. The first is an enemy who hates us bitterly, and the second, a friend who loves us dearly. A truth can quite often hurt, and rather than facing it, we live a lie. Every once in a while a friend has the guts to expose that lie. Instead of being grateful, we resent that person and we consider what he or she did reprehensible, and we often sever the friendship. Practicing forgiveness might bring to light the fact that our friend was trying to help us and not hurt us. It might help expedite our need to face up to a truth that we've been trying to avoid.

Reason Number 5 is the fact that forgiveness is a bridge over which we must pass ourselves.

A guru promised a scholar a revelation of greater consequence than anything contained in scripture. The scholar, as you might imagine, took the guru up on his offer. The guru said, "Go out into the rain and raise your head and arms heavenward. That will bring you the first revelation." The next day the scholar came to report, "I followed your advice and water flowed down my neck, and I felt like a perfect fool." "Well," said the guru, "for the first day that's quite a revelation, isn't it?"

Too often, we consider ourselves beyond foolishness. We consider ourselves paragons of virtue, unable to make a mistake or commit a wrongdoing. The truth, as that scholar discovered, is otherwise. We need to practice forgiveness because we're not angels, and many will be the times we will be in need of forgiveness.

Reason Number 4 is the fact that it's the only way we can ever realize honest and true peace.

When Leonardo da Vinci was painting the Last Supper, he became angry with a man and lashed out at him. He even threatened him. As he went back to his studio and tried to paint, ironically, the face of Jesus, he discovered he wasn't able to do so. There was too much anger and resentment brewing inside him. He had no choice but to put down his brushes and go find the man and ask his forgiveness. It was only then that he had the inner calm needed to paint the face of Jesus.

When we wrong someone or when someone wrongs us, like da Vinci, that anger, hurt, and resentment will brew inside us. And unless we find a way to practice forgiveness and reconciliation, unless we unload those feelings, that anger, hurt, and resentment will rob us of inner peace and, like da Vinci, it can't help but negatively affect the performance of our vocational duties.

Reason Number 3 is that forgiveness serves as a source of needed inspiration.

Robert Coles, the noted Harvard psychologist, was called to Montgomery, Alabama, back in the '60s to help a young black girl who each day was escorted by federal marshals to an all-white school. Each day, the eight-year-old girl, whose name was Ruby Bridges, would have to walk past parents and children who would taunt her and call her every name under the sun. Besides that, every day she received volumes of hate mail.

What flabbergasted Coles was how psychologically healthy she was after weeks of such an ordeal. He couldn't figure out how that could be until one day he noticed that whenever she walked past those taunting parents and children she would be saying something. He discovered that she did that every day. Questioning her as to what she was saying when she walked past the crowd, Ruby Bridges answered that she was praying. "What is it that you're praying?" asked Coles. "I'm praying: 'Father, forgive them, for they do not know what they do.' " Of all the clients Coles ever had, none inspired him as much as did Ruby Bridges.

Reason Number 2 as to why we should be practicing forgiveness is that it happens to be an element of healing.

Dr. Bernie Siegel says that whenever he visits elderly patients, he always whispers in their ear that their sins are forgiven. It's been his experience that many people see their illness or their trouble as a punishment for their sins. Even though it isn't so, the belief is there. Forgiveness thus becomes critical if any healing is to take place.

In case you've despaired that I'd ever get there, **Reason Number 1** as to why we should practice forgiveness is that God has forgiven and still forgives us.

I read[2] of an interview in which John Killinger, the renowned preacher, was being asked about the contrast between the Old Testament and the New Testament. In the Old Testament, God was seen as vengeful and vindictive, while in the New Testament God was seen as reconciling and forgiving. The interviewer wanted to know how and why God changed.

Killinger's response was classic. He said that God never changed at all. God was always loving, reconciling, and forgiving. Jesus was sent, and the New Testament was written as a way for God to get rid of and correct a bad reputation. Since God always forgives us, we, in turn, should forgive others.

There you have it. The top ten reasons why we should practice forgiveness. Suffice it to say, if you haven't practiced forgiveness, it's time you started.

---

1. Anthony Robbins, *Awaken the Giant Within* (New York: Simon & Schuster, 1991).

2. James W. Moore, *You Can Get Bitter or Better* (Nashville: Abingdon Press, 1989), p. 61.

Hobson's Choice

Scripture Lesson: Luke 1:26-48
... Let it be with me according to your word ...

It is difficult to accept the ambiguities of life. But accept them we must!

The British have an expression: "Hobson's Choice." It seems there was a certain man named Hobson who kept a livery stable in Cambridge somewhere around the seventeenth century. If you came to him to hire a horse, it was his rule that you took the one next to the door. If you didn't take that one, you'd get none at all. It is from this Hobson and his insistence on taking the horse next to the door that there came the phrase "Hobson's Choice." To be faced with Hobson's Choice means that you have no alternative, you must accept what is there.

One of the biggest difficulties in life is coming face to face with Hobson's Choice. Something bad happens. Something we wouldn't wish on our worst enemy occurs within our family. Something we'd just as soon not have to deal with demands our attention. Some disappointment, some misfortune, some pain, some awful tragedy comes our way. We'd like to pretend that it's all an illusion. We'd like to forget it, ignore it, or run away from it. But we can't. It's "Hobson's Choice." We have to accept it. We have no alternative.

There's a story about the mother of a family talking to John. She's telling him that he must go to school. "But I don't want to go!" he says. "You must!" she replies. He complains, "I don't want to, all the kids pick on me!" She says, "Never mind, you have to go to school!" He says, "I don't want to; all the teachers pick on me!" "Never mind," she says, "John, you are the principal, you have to go to school!"

When we're faced with the reality of "Hobson's Choice," we often feel like John. We're not very happy. Everything seems to be working against us. We long for an alternative, but there is none. School's in session and we're the principal. Sure, I suppose we could stay home, but it's not going to change anything. Sooner or later we have to accept our "Hobson's Choice" and make the best of it. To do otherwise means resigning from life, sitting at home in misery, heartache, bitterness, anger, and despair.

Take the "Hobson's Choice" in the death of a loved one. Our world is shattered. Our heart is broken. The pain is overwhelming. It's important and it's necessary that we grieve, and not just a few days, but often a few months and sometimes even a few years. But there comes a time when we must accept the death and move on with life.

I'm reminded of the story called "The Dark Candle" by Strickland Gillian.[1] The story is about a man who is incapable of functioning because of the death of his daughter. He just can't bring himself to do anything. One day he goes to sleep and dreams that he is in heaven where all the children are marching with lighted candles. He sees one child way down the line with a dark candle. So he runs to that child, and as he approaches her he realizes that it is his daughter. When he gets to her he says, "How is it, darling, that your candle is the only one that's unlighted?" She says, "Father, they often re-light it, but your tears always put it out."

When we lose someone we love to death, we can't keep putting out their candles with our tears. Eventually, we have to accept death and move on with life. To do otherwise is not helping us nor is it helping that person to achieve peace.

We find a similar thread in another "Hobson's Choice," that being a broken relationship. I've dealt on numerous occasions with men or women who have had a relationship die. Their pain and their grief is overwhelming, often more so than that of a relationship which was ended by a death. Be it a marriage or a long courtship, there's nothing that hurts more than the realization that what once was is now over. The man and the woman will spend endless hours berating themselves, spouting all sorts of "if only" litanies: "If only I had done this, if only I had done that, if only that didn't happen!" And what's worse, they'll fool themselves into thinking that one day they'll get back together again. I'm not discounting the possibility of reconciliation, but all too often the relationship is beyond that. Forgiveness is needed but it won't result in the rekindling of a love that is no longer there.

One thinks of Miss Havisham in Charles Dickens' *Great Expectations.* Jilted by her lover hours before the wedding, she lives the rest of her life in a darkened room with the wedding dress she was to be married in turning to rags upon her and her wedding cake moldering, uneaten among the cobwebs. Although she's a fictional character, and a caricature at that, Miss Havisham can stand for far too many who have experienced a broken relationship. They literally stop living, feeding endlessly on their own bitterness. Somewhere along the line they have to accept the fact that the relationship is over. They have to move on with their lives because not to do so will mean a life not much different from that of Miss Havisham.

Then there's the "Hobson's Choice" of a crippling handicap, something like that "thorn in the flesh" that Saint Paul talks about in his Letters. He prayed constantly that the thorn be taken away. But it wasn't. He had to live with it. He had to accept it. So must we if a crippling handicap comes our way.

There's a story about two men, both Italian sculptors and contemporaries, Michelangelo and Donatello. One day Donatello received a huge block of granite. After examining it carefully, Donatello rejected the marble because it was cracked and it had a hole in it. His studio was near Michelangelo's, and knowing how hard it would be to take the stone back to the quarry, the haulers decided to drop it off at Michelangelo's studio. He was absent-minded and they figured that he would think he ordered it. When Michelangelo inspected the marble, he saw the same cracks and the same hole that Donatello saw. But he also saw the block as a challenge to his artistic skills. So Michelangelo proceeded to carve from that seemingly worthless piece of granite what is considered to be one of the world's greatest art treasures, the statue of David.

When faced with the "Hobson's Choice" of a crippling handicap, we can practice denial. We can wish it or pray it away. But the fact of the matter is that it is there to stay. Like Saint Paul with his "thorn in the flesh" and like Michelangelo with his block of granite, we have to live with it, we have to accept it. It is then, and only then, that we can realize a new life, a new life that might produce a treasure greater than the statue of David, a new life that might be more saintly than that of Saint Paul.

Then there's the matter of getting help. There is nothing in the world that we have more difficulty in accepting than the fact that we need help. Having been raised in an environment of rugged individualism, having learned early in life to be self-sufficient, the very idea of not being able to make it on our own becomes repugnant.

There is a famous legend of the death of Roland, one of Charlemagne's inner circle. Along with his friend Oliver, he was the leader of the rear guard of Charlemagne's army. One day, he, Oliver, and their small band of warriors were suddenly surrounded by the Moors. Roland wore at his side a great horn whose blast could be heard miles and miles away. "Blow the horn," said Oliver, "and Charlemagne will come to our aid." But Roland refused. He was too proud to ask for help. The battle raged and Roland still refused to sound the call for help. One by one his men were slain until only he and Oliver were left. Oliver was slain and Roland was mortally wounded. Only then did he sound the call for help. Charlemagne arrived shortly thereafter only to find Roland and Oliver dead along with every one of the warriors.

Roland is like many of us. We'd rather die than ask for help. How awful and terrible it is that we'd rather ruin our family with our drinking or our drug use, that we'd rather stay in our misery, that we'd rather demonstrate our stupidity, that we'd rather jeopardize our job, our health, our future; how awful and how terrible that we'd rather do that than sound the horn for help, that we'd rather do that than accept the fact that we can't do it by ourselves anymore.

Then there's the matter of accepting reality. As much as we find asking for help repugnant to our nature, we also find change repugnant to our nature. We are not very accepting when it comes to doing things differently, and many times reality dictates that we do things differently.

A woman was suffering from extreme emotional anxiety. Her anxiety was the result of a recurring dream. Night after night she dreamed the same dream, awakening each morning with a terrible headache and complete exhaustion. Seeking help, she went to a psychiatrist. The doctor asked what it was that she dreamed. She answered, "Each night I dream that I'm trying to open a large door. I feel that it is important that I go in through the doorway. The door is a large glass one and there is a single word printed on it. All night I pull and pull at the door and it will not open. At the end of the dream, I am exhausted and I collapse at the foot of the door." After several minutes of deep thought, the psychiatrist asked, "What is the word that is printed on the door?" The woman answered, "The sign says 'push'!"

So often in life we are like that woman in that dream. We pull against reality. We refuse to accept the fact that we're too old and we can't do it any more, that we're too sick and we can't maintain the pace we're accustomed to, that we're too broke and we can't live high off the hog any more. We keep wanting to "pull" when the situation is now calling for us to "push."

In case you haven't guessed by now, I'm talking today about acceptance and how critical acceptance is to the carrying on of life. Our Gospel story today is a classic story of acceptance. Mary is facing an unbelievable challenge. She is with child and that child is to be the Son of God. And as much as she'd just as soon have had someone else bear that role, she realized that it was a "Hobson's Choice," that she had to do it, there was no alternative. She accepted it fully with those beautiful words, "I am the handmaid of the Lord, let it be done to me as you say."

Mary is our model and our inspiration when we're faced with "Hobson's Choice," when something happens to us for which there are no alternatives, for which as much as we'd like things to be different, they can't be different.

When we're faced with the death of a loved one or the death of a relationship, when we're faced with a crippling handicap or a need for help, when we're faced with the need to come up against a reality that we'd just as soon not face — cry, we must; grieve, we must; be angry, we must; be upset, we must. It is important and it is necessary to do all of the above for as long as it takes. But there comes a time for acceptance and, unless we come to grips with the necessity of that acceptance, we're destined for nothing but misery, pain, heartache, and despair. As Michelangelo proved and showed, that acceptance doesn't mean standing pat, it simply means making the best of life despite the cracks and holes in its structure.

Don't let your tears keep putting out the candles that your loved one in heaven is carrying! Don't be a Miss Havisham, a Donatello, or a Roland! Don't keep "pulling" when it's time to "push." Accept your "Hobson's Choice"! Get on with your life! Carve your statue of David!

---

1. Described by Bernie Siegel M.D., *How to Live Between Office Visits* (New York: Harper Collins, 1993), p. 223.

Purple Ribbon

Scripture Lesson: 1 John 3:1-2
... we are God's children now ...

In a lecture on the use of imagination in preaching, Doctor Ernest Campbell related an experience involving the late George Buttrick. While delivering his Thanksgiving sermon, Buttrick made note of a little girl's prayer. The prayer centered on the wish that God would take care of himself, after all there was much riding on his shoulders. Buttrick then solemnly exclaimed, "But, of course, God couldn't answer the little girl's prayer." Fully expecting to be told why the prayer couldn't be answered, Campbell listened very attentively. Buttrick, however, went on with the sermon. At the very end Buttrick addressed the "why" for which Campbell was anxiously waiting. As though it were an afterthought, Buttrick exclaimed: "And, of course, we know why God couldn't answer the little girl's prayer ... because God is love and love seeketh not its own." The why moved Ernest Campbell to tears.

I've always wanted to duplicate that piece of homiletic imagination on the part of George Buttrick. Here is my attempt at "hooking" the congregation with an opening story, the "why" of which will have to wait until the very end.

Long ago there was a woman who, in the company of people, had the habit of kneeling until everyone left. When people would ask her why she was kneeling, she would always respond that she was simply being faithful to the wishes of Pope Innocent III. So, if there were a party, there she would be on her knees talking with people and crawling on her knees for drinks or for food. If there were a concert, a play, or a sporting event, there she would be on her knees watching from an aisle. People in general didn't know what to make of it. Since Pope Innocent III lived a long time ago, people had no idea what his wishes had been, and so they hadn't the foggiest notion as to what would cause a seemingly sane and healthy woman to drop to her knees as often as she did. Many considered her an eccentric, a bit odd, maybe a bit unbalanced, but one thing was for sure — no one who saw her was untouched by her obvious state of happiness.

It's funny that many times in the course of life we encounter people like that, maybe not people who are on their knees all the time, but unusual people, odd or different people, people whose mannerisms, whose gestures, whose physical features are a bit out of the ordinary, people who might have some sort of handicap or defect. Unfortunately, in all too many cases we tend to distance ourselves from them, we tend to leave them with the impression that they are somehow a bit freakish and thus not candidates for the mainstream, not welcome at gatherings of regular people. All too often the people in question take that to heart and begin to doubt their very nature and they begin to see themselves as somewhat less than human, a sideshow on the stage of life.

Interesting enough, that was very much the story of Joseph Merrick, whose life was captured on stage and screen as the *Elephant Man*. Joseph Merrick suffered from neurofibromatosis, a disease for which there is no cure and which invariably ends in hideous disfigurement, pain, and premature death. And in nineteenth century London where Merrick grew up, the horror of neurofibromatosis was considerably compounded by a widespread though erroneous assumption that this sort of disorder began because of a moral lapse for which either the victim or his parents were responsible.

In any case, Joseph Merrick was discovered by Dr. Frederick Treves while Merrick was working as a freak in the sideshow of a second-rate circus. Merrick was barely able to speak, horribly deformed in body, hideous to look upon, forced to go about wearing a mask when not on display, and so crushed by the laughter of indifferent circus patrons that he had withdrawn almost completely within himself. Dr. Treves managed to get Joseph Merrick permanent residence at the London hospital where he worked as senior surgeon and lecturer in anatomy. Under the physician's care and through the efforts of many who took an interest in him, the real Joseph Merrick began to shine through the ungodly body in which he was encased. Money was collected to provide him with a tutor, books, and craft lessons. It wouldn't be long and Merrick would be regaling people with his knowledge of Shakespeare, his wit, his charm, and his beauty. He would unfortunately die shortly thereafter but not before feeling esteemed, special, and dignified. Merrick in the end was lucky. His humanity was rescued by Dr. Treves and so many others who were successful in reversing the long years of negative messages, years during which he was led to believe that his blip wasn't worth recording on the monitor of life. Unfortunately, for every happy ending like that of Joseph Merrick, there are countless others not as lucky, countless others who die feeling very much as though they are not of matter or importance to anybody, who die truly believing that they are or have become freakish non-persons, people of little value, worth, or significance. They may not have suffered from neurofibromatosis, but because of the circumstances and conditions of their lives, they share with Merrick the sense of rejection, the sense that they do not belong in the mainstream of life.

There are many here who can relate to that. Many of us have a bit of the early Joseph Merrick inside us. Maybe we're a little odd; maybe we're not that pretty; maybe we're sick or disabled, physically or mentally; maybe we're a little slower than the rest; maybe we're clumsy; maybe we're handicapped; maybe we're nerdy; maybe we're too short or maybe we're too tall; maybe we're too fat or maybe we're too skinny. And as we look at the world around us, we get the sense, sometimes real, sometimes imagined, that since we are somewhat flawed, our esteem and our value can't be very high, that we can't be very important, that the thing that's wrong with us disqualifies our ever being of much good no matter what we do.

There's a comic strip that used to appear periodically in the Sunday paper. Its prime character is a king who's obsessed with his shortness. Many of the laughs we get from reading the strip revolve around the king's efforts to prove he is a worthy monarch even though he is short. One strip had the king falling asleep and dreaming of ruling a nation of tiny people. They won his heart by calling him "Stretch," for that's exactly how he wanted to be seen.

The flaw in that particular comic character is not his shortness. The flaw is in his thinking that his worth as a king depends upon his size, that his value to the people he's ruling will be negatively affected because of his diminutive stature. That's the line of thinking that affects so many of us who have a bit of the early Joseph Merrick inside us. We have the mistaken notion that our particular flaw represents a barrier to our self-worth, that somehow or other that which makes us a bit different from others happens to negate our status as a worthwhile and important human being. Nothing could be further from the truth.

On more than one occasion, you've heard me rattle off from this pulpit a number of names of people of history who distinguished themselves, who are esteemed to this very day, even though they possessed a severe flaw. Beethoven was deaf when he wrote his great symphonies. Milton was blind when he wrote *Paradise Lost.* Grandma Moses was eighty years old when she started painting. Louis Pasteur was paralyzed from a stroke when he made his famous discoveries. Franklin Roosevelt ran our country for four terms from a wheelchair. Admittedly, they distinguished themselves by what they were able to produce, but they were able to produce because they did not deem their handicap, their flaw, as relegating them to a second-class status. Though society may have labeled them as misfits, though society may have left them with the impression that they were either too old or too crippled to be of any worth, they never let that label, that impression, take away from how they felt about themselves. Deep down inside they knew they were of worth and value despite what anybody said.

Two psychiatrists had offices in the same building. They often rode the same elevator together in the morning. The one who got off first invariably turned around and spat on his colleague. The other would pull out his handkerchief and wipe his face, his tie, and suit before getting off a few floors later. One morning the elevator operator could contain his curiosity no longer. As he was closing the door on the first psychiatrist, he said, "For heaven's sake, Doctor, tell me why your colleague does this to you!" The second psychiatrist calmly replied, "Oh, I don't know. That's his problem!"

Society may have spit on Beethoven or Milton or Grandma Moses or Franklin Roosevelt, informing them subtly or overtly that their handicap, their flaw, their physical oddity, made them useless human beings. But they saw the spit as society's problem, not theirs. They believed they were still valuable, still useful, still productive, still important, and too bad if everyone thought otherwise.

I'm reminded of Victor Frankl's famous line from his monumental work based on his experience in the concentration camps of Germany where Jews like himself were stripped of all dignity and were constantly told they were worthless and useless. In *Man's Search for Meaning,*[1] Frankl said that "everything can be taken from a man but one thing, and that's to choose one's attitude in any given circumstance, to choose one's way." And many Jews chose to hold their head high despite what happened to them, despite the way they were treated, despite the spit that may have showered down upon them.

That brings me at long last to the basis for the sermon. John, in our second reading, informs us that we are children of God, not children of Satan. As such we happen to have divine blood running through our veins. We are of dignity and status in God's eyes and nothing can take that away, no flaw, no oddity, no handicap. Saint Paul says in one of his Letters that nothing can separate us from God's love. In the same way, it can be said that nothing can separate us from the dignity which God bestowed on us by making us his children.

There was a teacher in the old days of France who tutored a prince, a person of royal blood. As a means of discipline in case the young boy stepped out of line and as a means for making sure he always held his head high, the teacher pinned a purple ribbon on the prince's tunic. She told him that the ribbon represented the royal purple of France. If he stepped out of line, if he held his head low, she'd point to the purple ribbon and make an appeal for him to live up to the dignity that was his by virtue of his royalty.

By calling us his children, God hung a purple ribbon on our tunics. It doesn't matter if we're too fat or too thin or too tall or too short or if we're odd or slow or handicapped. It doesn't matter if there is a bit of Joseph Merrick inside us. The purple ribbon is on our tunic and it can't be taken away. So what if Madison Avenue or society or some acquaintance spits out some insinuation that we're not special or important or of worth or value? Remember, it's their problem, not ours.

Joseph Merrick was lucky. Dr. Frederick Treves helped him to locate his purple ribbon. May you do the same for the Joseph Merricks you know. If you're feeling like the early Joseph Merrick, don't allow the laughter, the rejection, the feeling of inferiority to get you down. Remember, you're a child of God; you're wearing a purple ribbon.

By the way, in case you were wondering about the girl who was always found kneeling in the midst of people — someone finally asked her about Pope Innocent III's wishes which prompted her behavior. She said, "Long ago in the thirteenth century, Pope Innocent III confirmed a custom and made it a tradition. He said, 'When you come to church you should genuflect or go down on one knee. When you are in the presence of God, you must kneel down on both knees.' When I'm in the presence of people, I'm in the presence of God's children. I must kneel on both knees."

---

1. Victor E. Frankl, *Man's Search For Meaning* (New York: Simon & Schuster, 1959), p. 75.

Preferring The Lie To The Truth

Scripture Lesson: John 16:12-15
... When the Spirit of truth comes,
he will guide you into all the truth ...

Facing up to the truth can be very difficult.

One of the biggest challenges that a priest or minister faces is presiding at the funeral of someone whose life was far from exemplary. You'd like to say some good things about the deceased, but there is little if any good to be found.

A colleague of mine told me recently of a minister who was up against that dilemma. John Smith, who was an adulterer, a liar, a cheat, and a thief, was to be buried and his wife approached the minister about the funeral. She admitted to her husband's reprehensible life but wished the truth not be told. So she asked the minister if he could tell the congregation that her husband was a good man. He said, "I can't do that! I have to speak the truth!" "Look," she said, "I'll pay you $10,000 if you'll say he was a good man." The minister, not wanting to pass on the money, said, "Okay, if you insist." Now realizing his need to speak the truth and realizing his promise to the wife of the deceased, he embarked on an interesting strategy. Rising to the pulpit on the day of the funeral, he told the congregants, "My friends, we all know that John Smith was an adulterer, a liar, a cheat, and a thief, but, compared to his brother, he was a good man."

I begin on this humorous note because I'd like to talk with you today about truth and, in particular, why it is that we all have such a hard time accepting the truth, why we so often wish to avoid the truth. We can speculate all we want as to why the widow in my apocryphal story wanted her husband cast as a good man, but the fact is that she preferred the lie to the truth. I'm afraid that in far too many cases we, too, prefer the lie to the truth.

Sometimes, it is excusable. Sometimes when you look at what a person is dealing with, you can appreciate why a lie is preferred.

Linda Topf, in her book *You Are Not Your Illness,*[1] talks about her journey through the illness of multiple sclerosis. One of the hardest things about the illness for her was accepting its reality. She did not want to face the truth of the disease and so she did all she could to deny its reality. She found that it was only when she finally accepted the truth that she could proceed with her life.

We call that denial, and denial is common with any horrible disease or any horrible diagnosis. Not able or ready to face the truth, we slip into denial and that often serves us well until we can muster the inner resources necessary to deal with the bad news. In due time, and sometimes the time can be long, we face the truth and, like Linda Topf, only then can we go on with life.

So there are cases where people prefer the lie to the truth, and it's excusable and we can appreciate the preference. But I'm afraid that in most cases people prefer the lie to the truth, and it is not excusable because we're not dealing with illness or disease or a bad diagnosis. We're dealing with a general unwillingness to face up to the responsibilities, the revelations, and the changes which the truth requires.

A minister was called to a church and was warned that the church is dead. Nevertheless, he regarded the call as a challenge and he decided to accept it. He soon discovered that the church was dead. No planning, no toil, no exhortation, no urging could kindle a spark of life or awaken any response. He told the congregation of that discovery and he proposed to have a funeral for the church. A day was fixed. A coffin was brought into the church. The walls were decorated with mourning wreaths. When the time of the burial service came, the church was packed. It hadn't been that crowded in years. The minister did a lovely job with the service. Then at the end, as a last token of respect, he invited the congregation to file past the open coffin. As they did so, they received a shock. The coffin was open and empty but the bottom of the coffin was not wood. It was glass, it was a mirror. As people looked into the coffin, they saw their own faces.

The pastor used the burial service to bring home a truth no one wanted to accept, the truth that all their fingers of blame were pointed in every direction but the right one. The church was dead because the people had died. It was not someone else's fault, it was their own fault.

Now that's a typical truth many of us have a hard time swallowing. We're big on blaming and complaining but we're not big on responsibility. We're big on laying the cause for a problem or a misery onto shoulders other than our own.

I like that story about the two painters on their lunch break. One of them looks into his lunch box and protests, "Peanut butter, peanut butter, peanut butter, I hate peanut butter. I can't take another day of it!" His partner inquires: "Why don't you ask your wife to make you something else?" "Oh, I'm not married," said the first painter, "I make my own sandwiches."

How often has it happened that we complained about something; we expressed our dismay over something; we stewed over something; yet it lay within our capacity and power to do something about it. It was well within our means to change what had to be changed, to restore what had to be restored. It was well within our capacity to make sandwiches other than peanut butter. But that meant commitment, that meant responsibility, that meant work, and we weren't willing to assume any of the three. So rather than face that truth and accept that fact, we go instead with the lie and we keep right on blaming, complaining, and protesting.

You have the matter of embarrassment. We sometimes prefer the lie to the truth because the truth would mean our admitting to something we'd just as soon not admit.

Robert McNamara, the former Secretary of Defense, practically admitted in his latest book that that was one of the tragic realities of the Vietnam War. The powers that be knew the war was wrong; the powers that be knew the war was unwinnable; the powers that be knew they should get out. But instead of admitting the truth and confessing the error, the powers that be went with the lie, and I need not outline the horrible ramifications of that lie.

How often has it happened that we've done the same, that we've not faced the truth, that we've gone along with the lie, because we couldn't stand the embarrassment of admitting we were wrong, of admitting we were dishonest, of admitting we were stupid, of admitting that we, of all people, were capable of sin.

Then there is the matter of change. People will prefer the lie to the truth in many instances because to face the truth is to face change. I needn't tell you how much we dislike change.

I'd like to share with you a vignette from one of Anthony De Mello's books.[2] It's titled "The Ashram Cat":

> *When the Guru sat down to worship each evening the ashram cat (who had wandered in from the outside) would get in the way and distract the worshipers. So he ordered that the cat be tied during evening worship.*

> *After the Guru died the cat continued to be tied during evening worship. And when the cat expired, another cat was brought to the ashram so that it could be tied during evening worship.*

> *Centuries later learned treatises were written by the Guru's scholarly disciples on the liturgical significance of tying up a cat while worship is performed.*

Many of our habits which we view as sacred, many practices which we proclaim as the way it's supposed to be, many practices which we refuse to abandon are like the tying up of that ashram cat. The whole basis behind it is silly. It might have made sense a long time ago, but it makes no sense now. But rather than accept the truth and give in to the change, we continue to tie up our ashram cat and hold fast to the lie of its relevance, importance, and sacredness.

We prefer the lie to the truth to avoid responsibility. We prefer the lie to the truth to avoid embarrassment. We prefer the lie to the truth to avoid change. We also prefer the lie to the truth because the truth involves our admission that we are powerless.

How often have you heard people say that they're in complete control of things, that they can quit smoking or drinking or gambling or drugs any time they want? How often have you heard people say that, when it's obvious to everyone but themselves that it's simply not true? It's a lie that has destroyed thousands of lives, and it stems from a person's unwillingness to claim the truth of his or her powerlessness.

That's the beauty of the twelve-step programs. People admit they're not as powerful as they thought they were, that their addiction is out of their control. It's only when they can face up to that truth that any hope of rehabilitation is possible.

There's a psychiatrist in Brazil who suggests that the most common human mental illness is what he calls theomania: the delusion that we human beings can be God, that we can be the scriptwriter for our life. That lie not only results in resistance to the reality of addiction but it also results inevitably in anger, depression, and self-blame when life doesn't turn out as expected.

In my work with people who have experienced a tragedy, one of the hardest nuts to crack is the idea on the part of the grievers that had they been present, the tragedy wouldn't have occurred — had they been there somehow or another, death would have been held at bay. Sometimes you get the opposite reaction in which people feel they were the cause of the tragedy — they were responsible for the death of their loved one. Although in some cases there may be some truth in that line of thinking, in the overwhelming majority of cases there is no truth to it at all and the hardest thing to accept on the part of grievers is the truth that they were powerless to do anything about the tragedy or about the death of that loved one.

There is also the matter of comfort and security. People will choose to stay with the lie; they will prefer the lie, because admitting to the truth would be too disruptive of their lives and their lifestyle.

I'm reminded of the story of a Peace Corps worker trying to convince a native of India not to drink from the Ganges River because of its high degree of pollution. To demonstrate the truth of what he was saying he took a microscope and put a drop of water under its lens. There, as clear as day, were all sorts of germs floating in every direction. He then asked the Indian to look into the microscope to see the germs, hoping that by seeing them he would quit drinking the water. His reaction was classic. The Indian took his cane and smashed the microscope into pieces. The thought of drinking water elsewhere was not a thought he wanted to entertain. It would mean a major disruption of his lifestyle and life habits. So he figured that by getting rid of the microscope, he'd get rid of the truth and stay with the lie.

We can laugh at that, but consider how we're often guilty of doing the very same thing. We don't smash microscopes with our canes but what we do in its place is mentally to shred the many medical reports indicating that the food we're eating and the lifestyle we're leading can be hazardous to our health. Rather than disrupt our lives with change, we prefer to stay with the lie that our present eating and living habits won't do us any harm.

In our Gospel today, Jesus tells his disciples and he tells us that the Spirit of truth will guide us to all truth. I firmly believe the Spirit is constantly doing that, but we offer heavy resistance.

The Spirit is guiding us to a mirror where we might find the real source of the pain and trouble we're in, but we prefer blaming and complaining. The Spirit is guiding us towards an admittance of our error, an admittance of our mistake, but we can't or won't handle the embarrassment. The Spirit is guiding us to make a change, but we insist on tying up our ashram cat. The Spirit is guiding us away from theomania, but we keep coming back to the illusion that we're in control of our addictions, that we could have done something about the tragedy. The Spirit is guiding us to a recognition of our terrible lifestyle, our terrible eating habits, but we decide to break the microscope and mentally shred any evidence of the truth.

Jesus said the Spirit of truth will guide us to the truth. May we all give up our preference for the lie and give in to the guidance of that Spirit.

---

1. Linda Noble Topf, *You Are Not Your Illness* (New York: Simon & Schuster, 1995).

2. Anthony De Mello, *The Song of the Bird* (Garden City, N.Y.: Image Books, 1982), p. 63.

Antidotes For "Perfectionism"

Scripture Lesson: Mark 6:7-13
... shake off the dust that is on your feet ...

It is one thing to seek perfection but it is another thing to make it an obsession.

A man was searching for the perfect wife. He moved in circles where he could meet a lot of women and every once in a while he came upon someone whom he thought fit the bill, only to discover that she wasn't quite up to snuff. One could cook, but her looks weren't all that great. One was pretty, but she wasn't all that wholesome. One was talented, but her personality left much to be desired. Finally, he came upon someone whom he deemed the perfect wife. He was ecstatic. His search was finally over. With great haste, he asked her to marry him. To his great horror, she refused. When he asked her why, she said it was simple. She was looking for the perfect husband.

That story, told by Doctor Bernie Siegel, touches upon something about which we're often preoccupied — perfection. Far too many of us have an intense notion that we have to be perfect, that everything has to be perfect, that we can't make a mistake, that to fail is anathema, that winning is everything. Certainly it's admirable and good that we seek perfection, but unfortunately for many of us it has become an obsession; it has made us intolerant of mistakes or failures in ourselves or in others. Here are some antidotes to the growing disease of "perfectionism."

First of all we need to realize that perfection is beyond us. Antique oriental carpets have a small flaw woven into them by their Muslim makers. They purposely leave a stitch undone because perfection, they say, belongs only to God. Orthodox Jews leave a small patch unpainted in a freshly painted room because they believe to be perfect is not of this world. Because those are practices not of our culture, we seldom have that point driven home to us as often

63

as it should be. The reality is that perfection is indeed reserved for God.

Secondly, we need to remember that things of exquisite beauty, things we call great, are often not perfect. Not too long ago in Detroit, two Rembrandt paintings were shown. One of the local reviewers said that he thought one of them was a fake. Experts were called to examine it, and it was determined that one picture was in fact a fake, not a genuine Rembrandt. When the experts were asked how they could arrive at that conclusion, they said, "Well, when Rembrandt painted, there were many mistakes in his pictures which he then covered over. There were no mistakes in the one we looked at. It was too perfect to be a Rembrandt."

We often deem masterpieces as perfect paintings, but the reality is that although they may seem perfect at first glance, a closer examination will often reveal the little mistakes the painter covered over before unveiling the finished product.

That leads to the third antidote for "perfectionism." Anyone who has achieved any success in life, anyone who has achieved any sort of alleged perfection in life, did so only on the heels of multiple mistakes and failures.

A story is told about a boy named Sparky. For Sparky, school was all but impossible. He failed every subject in the eighth grade. He flunked physics in high school. Receiving a flat zero in the course, he distinguished himself as the worst physics student in the school's history. Sparky also flunked Latin, Algebra, and English. He didn't do much better in sports. Although he did manage to make the school's golf team, he promptly lost the only important match of the season. There was a consolation match. He lost that, too. You could call Sparky a first-class loser, and so he was tabbed by those who knew him.

Now Sparky had one talent, and he knew it. That was drawing. Not letting the loser label get him down, he pursued a career in drawing, only to meet with further failure. One studio after another rejected his drawings. Finally he received some interest from Walt Disney who suggested that he draw a series of cartoons. He did so, but they were ultimately rejected. Exasperated but undaunted, he decided to write his own autobiography in cartoon. He described his childhood self, a little boy loser. He sent it to a publisher who decided to print it. The cartoon character would soon become famous worldwide. Sparky, the boy who failed every subject in grade school, was none other than Charles Schulz; the cartoon boy he painted was Charlie Brown of *Peanuts* fame whose kite never could fly and who never seemed to succeed in kicking a football.

And if you think Charles Schulz had a track record of failure and rejection, check out this person's dossier:

> *When he was 22 years old, a business he started went broke. The following year he tried his hand at politics but was defeated in his attempt to win a seat in the state legislature. He attempted again to start a business. It failed. The following year he finally was elected only to have a girl he was fond of and planning to marry get sick and eventually die. He lost his re-election bid.*

I could go on with other failures and rejections. The person I'm talking about is Abraham Lincoln, one of the greatest presidents this nation has ever known.

Of course, we all know that elderly gentleman who drove around the country sleeping in his car looking for someone to back him in a business venture. He received 1,009 "no's," before he finally got a "yes." It was then that Colonel Sanders opened up a restaurant that sold fried chicken. If you were to pull the files on the most successful people this country has known, you would find a track record of multiple mistakes and failures.

That leads to the fourth antidote for "perfectionism" — the realization that it is far better to risk a mistake or to chance a failure than it is to be perfect or successful.

A few years ago, Thomas Peters and Robert Waterman went exploring America's best-run companies. They would later pen the book *In Search of Excellence*.[1] One of their paradoxical discoveries was that those companies which are most demanding of success and least tolerant of failure are companies with rather mediocre records. The best-run companies, on the other hand, encourage failure. One top-rated CEO had among his commandments for employees: "Make sure you generate a reasonable amount of mistakes." Think about it: If nine out of ten experimental products are failures, the company must generate 27 blunders to place three profitable products on the market.

Carrying that thought to another area of competition, think for a moment about that famous "Dream Basketball Team" of the 1992 Olympics when Magic Johnson, Larry Bird, Michael Jordan, and a whole host of NBA all-stars rolled over all the competition. They had a perfect record. They were successful. They won the gold. But I doubt if many of us thought much about that success or perfection. Their competition was a joke. There was no team they couldn't destroy without working up a sweat. We would have thought more of them if they played talent of similar caliber and lost.

Some of us have never failed. We've been perfect. But that is only because we have not attempted much, only because we've never been stretched. Like that "Dream Team," all of our accomplishments have been well within our capability. Some of us would be better human beings if we failed, if we had given our efforts to something beyond our reach, if we had given our efforts to something so demanding that it took all we had and then asked for more. Yes, it is far better to risk a mistake, to chance a failure, than it is to be perfect or successful. At least you can hold your head high.

The fifth antidote for "perfectionism" is keeping things in perspective. The Buffalo Bills are about to break training camp and isn't it a pity that so many people only seem to dwell on the four Super Bowl losses and not the tremendous achievement of getting there four consecutive times. We have a bad habit of obsessing over a failure and not seeing all that was accomplished over and above the failure.

M. Scott Peck talks about his counseling sessions with people who have divorced after a long marriage. He says they always have a habit of thinking themselves a failure. They berate themselves for having made the wrong choice of a mate. They feel that all those years have been wasted. What Peck tries to remind them is that they leave their marriage with far greater mental and psychological strength than when they began their marriage. They learned to become loving parents to children with whom they still have a good relationship. Although they may have failed, a lot of good was accomplished.

That brings me at long last to the inspiration for my antidotes to perfectionism, and that's our Gospel. Jesus is sending his disciples out to preach the gospel. In his instructions he tells them up front not to expect perfection. He says there will be towns and villages where they're going to flop, where they will bungle the operation, where things aren't going to go well. He said if that happens, "Don't worry about it! It's not the end of the world. Shake the dust from your feet and move on." What he wanted his disciples to realize is that it's okay to strike out in their efforts to preach the gospel.

For all you perfectionists out there, we welcome your thirst for perfection, but if it's gone too far, here are some antidotes: First of all, keep uppermost in your minds the fact known by Muslim carpet makers and Jewish painters — true perfection is beyond this world. It is reserved only for God. Second, remember that things of exquisite beauty, things labeled great, often are not perfect. If a painting is too perfect, it can't be a Rembrandt. Third, realize that the Charles Schulzs, the Abraham Lincolns, the Colonel Sanders of this world, those who have enjoyed much success, realize that most, if not all, have had track records of multiple mistakes and failures and rejections. Fourth, if you're obsessed with perfection, remember that it is better to risk a failure, to chance a mistake, than it is to be perfect or successful. Companies which enjoy excellence today live by that standard. People who can lift their heads high are more often those who have tried and failed than those whose success comes easy. Fifth, keep things in perspective. Don't discount the work and achievement prior to the failure. Lastly, remember that when all is said and done, you'll make your mark not by whether or not you were perfect but on how you lived your life.

Harry Emerson Fosdick put it well when he compared men and women to flagstaffs. Some flagstaffs are very tall and prominent, and some are small, but the glory of a flagstaff is not its size but the colors that it flies. A very small flagstaff flying the right colors is far more valuable than a very tall one with the wrong flag. When a man or woman is altogether done with life, the most satisfying thing would be the ability to say, "I'm ashamed that I was not a better, taller, straighter, more perfect flagstaff, but I'm not ashamed of the colors that I flew."

It is okay to seek perfection, but it is not okay to be obsessed with perfection. You're going to make mistakes and you're going to fail. Live with that reality. Shake the dust from your feet and move on. Remember, God is not interested in your won and lost record; God is interested in the colors that you fly.

---

1. Thomas Peters and Robert Waterman, *In Search of Excellence* (New York: Harper & Row, 1982).

Jesus Christ Or Arnold Palmer

Scripture Lesson: John 17:11-19

... that they also may be sanctified in truth ...

A talk for those pretending or attempting to be somebody that they are not.

———————————

There is a joke making the banquet circles that concerns two great beings, Jesus and Moses, out playing a round of golf. Jesus tees up at a long par three, two hundred yard hole. He sizes up the golf bag and chooses a three iron. Moses shakes his head doubtfully. "Jesus, it is a long hole. You'll never make it over the water with an iron, better use a wood." Jesus smiles and replies, "Arnold Palmer does it." Then he hits the ball with a resounding whack and it lands right in the middle of a big water hazard. Moses is feeling forgiving and offers to shag the ball and give his friend another crack at it. So Moses saunters to the water hazard and, with great aplomb, parts the waters and picks out the ball. Jesus tees up once again, and again he takes the three iron. Moses laments, "Jesus, you have already tried that iron. Believe me, the hole is too long. Here's a wood." Jesus patiently shakes his head and steps up to the ball. "Arnold Palmer does it," he says. Then he hits it and, of course, the ball falls short, landing once again in the water. This time he motions to Moses to stay put and he goes to shag the ball himself. He approaches the hazard, walks across the water and picks out the ball. Meanwhile the next foursome has caught up from behind and is looking on, astonished. "Who does he think he is?" asks one man, "Jesus Christ?" "No," says Moses sadly, "unfortunately, he thinks he's Arnold Palmer."

I tell you that story not to get laughs but to begin reflecting on a phenomenon that strikes far too many people. There are many who go through life trying to be somebody they're not. There are many people who lead lives of quiet desperation because their lives are not reflective of nor accepting of their true selves.

69

One of the great dramas of all time is Arthur Miller's *Death of a Salesman*.[1] It's the story of Willie Loman, a tragic figure who spends his entire life trying to be a hotshot salesman. He wants to go down in the history books as someone noted for making the most profitable of deals. He fails miserably, and at the end of the play he dies. The fact was that his real talent lay elsewhere. He was a gifted carpenter and craftsman, evidenced by the front porch of the family home, a product and testimony to his great talent. As the play draws to a close, his son speaks to the fact that there was more of Willie in that front porch than in any one of the sales he might have made. The tragedy of the play was that Willie Loman chose the wrong dream.

All too often the Willie Loman story repeats itself in real life. People end up choosing a career or profession that fails to speak to what lies within them. Whether it be pressure from parents or pressure from society, they put themselves into a line of work, into the fulfillment of a dream, that never reflected who they really were.

Several years back there was a resident doctor who was anything but thrilled about performing his duties. He was at the top of his class in medical school, but the accomplishment didn't mean much to him. He found the practical applications of his education and the grind of residency to be anything but exciting. One day, I happened to run into him in the parking lot and I saw that he was driving an antique car. When I made a few queries as to its make and model, he lit up in a way that I had never seen before. From his conversation I could see where his real passion lay.

I can't speak from any fact, but I wondered if he wasn't a doctor only because that was what his parents wanted him to be. I wondered if he pursued medicine because that was a profession laden with prestige, because that was a profession on which society pasted the label of success. I never saw that resident happy at his work and I believe that a good deal of that came from the fact that he chose the wrong dream. He entered a line of work that didn't speak to the real gifts and real passions that lay inside him.

If we are to make a case for honest living — for being ourselves instead of Arnold Palmer — we have to be sure that we are chasing the right dreams, that we are not fooling ourselves as to our talents and abilities and desires. We have to be sure that there is a direct connection between what is inside us and what we happen to be doing.

Another component of honest living rests in our ability to resolve the tension between who we would like to be and who we are. All too many of us would like to be a hero, a superstar, a giant, a figure of enormous talent, but the fact of the matter is, quite often, we are not.

Elie Wiesel, in his book *Souls on Fire*,[2] tells us that when we die and go to Heaven and meet our Maker, our Maker is not going to say to us, "Why didn't you become a Messiah?" "Why didn't you discover the cure for such and such?" The only thing we are going to be asked at that precious moment is "Why didn't you become you?"

Contrary to what Abraham Lincoln said, all of us were not created equal; some were endowed with many talents, some were endowed with a few. It doesn't matter where we fit into the spectrum of talents, we are equally loved by God and equally vital to his Kingdom. We can choose to go through life bemoaning the fact that we are not as good or as beautiful or as talented as the next person. We can choose to go through life falsely believing that we are as good and as beautiful and as talented as the next person. Or we can choose to go through life honoring the goodness, the beauty, and the talent we do have, celebrating the particular endowments that God has provided us and no other.

Robert Henri was an American portrait and landscape painter. He specialized in the portraits of children. On one occasion, Henri went to a New York art gallery for a private showing of his paintings. As he was admiring a portrait of John Singer Sargent, another famous painter, Henri heard the man next to him say, "At last, they've given me a place." Not wanting to ignore the proud statement of the stranger, Henri asked the man which of the paintings was his. Pointing proudly at the painting hanging before him, the stranger replied, "That one." "But John Sargent painted that one," Henri replied. "Yes," the stranger answered, "I think John Sargent did paint the picture, but I made the frame."

Maybe we can't paint a lovely picture, but we can do other things equally as beautiful. We'd like to be John Sargent or Arnold Palmer or Michelangelo, but their talents or abilities may not be ours. The ones we possess might have us accomplish things they could never hope to accomplish. We must be true to whom we are and whom we are capable of becoming. We can be as proud at making the frame as the artist is of making the painting. As Elie Wiesel pointed out, "You becoming You is all that God hopes you ever accomplish."

Another component of honest living is coming to grips with and accepting the handicaps, the faults, the flaws which are prevalent in all of our lives.

A man who took great pride in his lawn found himself with a large crop of dandelions. He tried every method he knew to get rid of them, but still they plagued him. Finally, he wrote to the Department of Agriculture. He enumerated all the things he had tried and he closed the letter with the question: "What shall I do now?" In due course, the reply came: "We suggest that you learn to love them."

Certainly we all have flaws and faults that can and should be overcome. But there are many that can't, and we have to live with them, we have to accept them, we have to love them. Whether it be lameness or blindness or neurosis or poverty or whatever; whether our limitations have been acquired or inherited, their existence has to be acknowledged and worked with. We have to learn to love them and, if not love them, at least accept them.

Louis Pasteur had a paralyzing stroke at age 46 and was handicapped for life. Beethoven was struck with deafness early in his career. Milton, the great poet, was blind. Van Gogh wrestled with mental illness for most of his life. In all of these cases, those great men went on to produce magnificence and beauty. They provided humanity with many wonderful and enriching gifts. And they did it all by loving their dandelions, by accepting their handicaps, their faults, their flaws and forging ahead with their lives despite them.

There are many cases where the very thing that limits a life turns out to be the spark that sets that life on fire. Handicaps and flaws that may be dreadful sometimes become the driving force behind a change in direction or a change in focus that will flush out talent and abilities one may have never known he or she had.

Immanuel Kant suffered all his life from a restricted chest which kept him in almost constant pain. One may conjecture that he would never have been the philosopher he was had he not faced or accepted his limitations. By doing so, he pointed his life in a direction where those limitations wouldn't stand in the way. "While I felt oppressed in my chest," he said, "my head was clear."

Robert Louis Stevenson came to that same realization. An illness that kept him confined to a bed pushed him into writing. We know the wonderful books that came as a result of that writing. By accepting and loving and coming to grips with that which they couldn't control, Kant and Stevenson were inspired to make the best of their lives over which they did have control.

Harry Fosdick put it best when he compared life to a landscape job. God hands us each a plot of land that may be ample or small, rugged or flat, picturesque or commonplace. One might not be able to eliminate some of the ugly features in the plot, but one can landscape the area in such a way that the ugliness will not only be missed but it may even be that which makes the site beautiful. Honest living requires that we learn to love and accept the existence of the dandelions and that we make the best of our lives despite them, or even because of them.

If we are to make a case for honest living —for being ourselves instead of Arnold Palmer — we have to choose the right dream. We have to respect who we are and not bemoan who we are not. We have to accept the handicaps, the faults, the flaws in our lives that can't be changed.

When Jesus in our Gospel prayed that the disciples be consecrated in truth, he wanted them to be who they truly were. He wanted them to be true to the talents and abilities and passions that each of them possessed. He wanted them to be true to the mission and goals that discipleship required. He wanted truth to set them free to be honest and genuine, not trying to be Arnold Palmer, but just the beautiful persons whom God had destined them as well as us to be.

So accept the plot of land God has given you to landscape. Don't jump over the fence to the next person's yard. Don't be concerned about the fact that your property may not be as good as your neighbor's. Learn to love the dandelions and make beautiful that which God has given you.

---

1. Arthur Miller, *Death of a Salesman* (New York: Penguin Books, 1977).

2. Elie Wiesel, *Souls on Fire* (Northvale, N.J.: Jason Aronson Inc., 1993).

The Answer Must Be
In The Form Of A Question

Scripture Lesson: Luke 11:9-11
> ... *Ask and it will be given you; search, and you will find; knock, and the door will be opened for you ...*

Sometimes questions are more important than answers.

One of the most popular and longest-running game shows on television is called *Jeopardy*. I can remember watching it when I was a kid. Art Fleming was the host back then. For some reason it was put into mothballs for several years but then it came back with a fury. Alex Trebek took over as host, and it has been a mainstay of evening television ever since.

Jeopardy features six categories of answers, and the object of the game is to come up with questions that properly coincide with the answers. Of the three contestants, the one who comes up with the most correct questions wins.

The questions we ask or don't ask can impact us in significant ways, and not only us, but the people around us as well. Just as the correct questions score big in *Jeopardy*, so do correct questions score big in life.

Let's take as a starter the matter of tragedy. Rare is the life that isn't tinged by its share of tragedy. Often the questions asked on the heels of a tragedy significantly affect that life.

In his best-selling book *When Bad Things Happen to Good People*,[1] Rabbi Harold Kushner tells of Martin Gray, a survivor of a Warsaw ghetto and the Holocaust. Martin Gray, after the Holocaust, rebuilt his life. He became successfully married and raised a family. Life seemed good after the horror of the concentration camp. Then one day his wife and children were killed when a forest fire ravaged their home in the South of France.

Gray was distraught, pushed almost to the breaking point by this added tragedy. People urged him to demand an inquiry into what caused the fire, but instead he chose to put his resources into a movement to protect nature from future fires. He explained that an inquiry, an investigation, would focus only on the past, on issues of pain, sorrow, and blame. He wanted to focus on the future.

In essence, Gray could have asked a lot of questions after the tragedy. He could have asked, "Why me? Who was responsible for the fire? Whom can I blame? Whom can I sue?" He could have asked, "Why do bad things keep happening to me? Why did God do this to me?" But he knew that all those questions would lead only to sadness, bitterness, anger, and vengeance. He chose to ask different questions instead. He asked, "Now that this has happened, what can I do? How can I rebuild my life? How can I make sure something good comes out of this awful experience?" By asking those kinds of questions, he could move on with life and prevent that tragedy from continuing to emit its poison.

That is an important lesson for all of us who might have to face the death of a loved one, the onslaught of some disease, the loss of a job, the curse of a handicap. We can ask empowering questions or disempowering questions. We can ask the proverbial "Why me?" question till we're blue in the face or, like Martin Gray, we can ask what it is we can do to make something good come from the tragic turn of events. In that way we can forge a positive future.

Then there's the matter of asking questions that help put things in perspective. These might be called inventory questions.

The late Dr. Bruce Thielemann once had someone come to his office who told him that the worst possible thing in the world had happened. Before he had a chance to say what it was, Thielemann asked him whether his wife had died. He said, "No! She's fine." "Then," asked Thielemann, "one of your kids must have been killed." "No," he said, "they're doing quite well." "I suppose your house burned down," said Thielemann. "No," he said, "it's in great shape. I just made the last mortgage payment." "Gee, I'm sorry that you've been diagnosed with a bad disease," said Thielemann. "No, no," he said, "my health is perfect."

There was, of course, a method to the madness of Dr. Thielemann. Before the gentleman had a chance to tell about the worst thing in the world that had happened, Thieleman, through questions, established for the gentleman that there were a lot of good things going on in his life. This most horrible thing in the world, which turned out to be the failure of his business, had sunk him to the depths of despair. A good deal of the sinking came from his failure to account for all the positives in his life that were still there despite the failed business.

That is another question that can be empowering when bad times come: the question of what we have going for us in spite of the trouble, in spite of the hardship, in spite of the bad news. We need to ask those types of inventory questions so that things are placed in their proper perspective. We also need to ask inventory questions before the trouble, before the hardship, before the bad news. The failure to do so can lead to our discovery too late that what we thought was so important really wasn't.

A well-known author of children's books was so busy doing well and becoming famous that he had no time for his little girl. When she unexpectedly died, he knew an anguish of sorrow and remorse that was unbelievable. She had often asked him, "Would you play with me?" But he seldom had the time to do so. Other matters occupied his attention. Now he declared that he would willingly surrender everything, all the wealth he had accumulated, all the success he had achieved, for one glimpse of her dear eyes and an opportunity to play her small games with her.

Had he asked, just once, the inventory question, "What is really important in life?" perhaps he wouldn't be so deeply pained with regrets and remorse. So often we find out too late that we put all our eggs in the wrong basket, that we worried into the night over things which, in hindsight, were of little value or of little importance or of little worth.

We need to ask inventory questions not only when trouble strikes but also before it strikes. In realizing where the real blessings and the real treasures of life lie, we might not be so easily sidetracked by what may seem important, necessary, and valuable but which pales in comparison to what is really important, really necessary, and really valuable.

Another category might be inquisitive questions. History has recorded many examples of wonderful things which have entered life because someone had been inquisitive enough to ask the why of something which everyone else apathetically accepted or endured without question.

George De Mestral was taking a stroll one day in his native Switzerland. Upon arriving home, he found his jacket covered with cockleburs, those things that stick to your clothes when you walk through brush. Picking the sticky pods off his clothes, De Mestral wondered what act of natural engineering could account for their tenacious sticking ability. Whereas you or I might curse the darned cockleburs for being a nuisance, De Mestral asked how they were able to attach themselves to clothing.

Taking out his microscope, he looked closely at their structure and noticed that they were covered with little hooks that entangled themselves in the loops of fabric in his jacket. As he studied that structure, he asked the further question of if and how that structure could be translated into something useful. The end result of the question was the invention of velcro.

Many grand and wonderful inventions have entered into life because there have been people who have asked inquisitive questions, who have asked why and how things are the way they are. The result of those questions has been that something practical and helpful and innovative has become a reality.

Asking inquisitive questions might not yield such wonderful results. They may not propel us onto the Who's Who list of inventors. But who is to say that the knowledge gained won't be helpful? Who is to say that such questions might not be useful or helpful in a somewhat different way? Many have been embarrassed or should be embarrassed because they took for granted something that needed a few questions.

A colleague of mine told of a high school reunion where one of his classmates was well dressed and looked rather wealthy. This immediately caused those who were out of earshot to snicker as to her appearance. "Did you see those shoes? Look at the handbag! Look at the rings! Get a look at the dress. Boy, is she uppity! Who does she think she is?"

My colleague went up to her and struck up a conversation asking her about her life. To his great surprise, she told a tale of woe. Her husband, who was also a graduate from that school, had died a few years before, a drowning victim of a hurricane. Shortly afterward their nineteen-year-old daughter, their only child, went into her room and took a gun and ended her life. As she told her story, tears ran down her cheeks.

How often has it happened that we've passed judgment, that we've made some fairly big assumptions, without ever bothering to ask questions to verify those judgments or those assumptions? Many of us have been cruel and have done others a disservice by taking for granted what we should have questioned.

On a lighter note, I once heard a story about a first grade teacher who was having a horrible day. It hadn't stopped raining, and 37 first graders had been cooped up in a small classroom the whole six hours with no recess. The children were absolutely wild. She had done all in her power to keep them calm. Finally, the clock indicated it was time to go home. With the rain still falling she began the arduous task of getting the right raincoats, the right rainhats, and the right boots on the right children.

She got all of them ready except for a six-year-old who had a pair of boots that were impossible to get on his feet. The teacher pushed and pulled and yanked until finally they slipped on. But then the little boy said: "Teacher, you know what? Those boots aren't mine!" The teacher wanted to scream but she didn't. She said a quick prayer, took a deep breath, and then began the difficult process of getting the boots back off. She pulled and she tugged and she yanked and finally they came off. Then the little boy said, "Teacher, they're my sister's boots, but she lets me wear them."

Asking questions can save not only a lot of embarrassment and a lot of false judgments, but it can save a lot of aggravation as well.

In our Gospel today, we find the classic expression of Jesus: "Ask and you shall receive, seek and you shall find, knock and the door will be opened to you." In essence, he's informing us that not only should we not be afraid to ask questions and seek answers, but that we should see that as an imperative if we ever hope to find entrance through the doors of his Kingdom.

Whether it be asking empowering questions or inventory questions or inquisitive questions, there's much to be gained in the practice. Like Martin Gray, asking empowering questions following a tragedy can keep us from getting mired in the mud of grief. Like the gentleman who came to Dr. Thielemann for help, like the author of those children's books, asking inventory questions can help us keep things in perspective and it can keep us from forever regretting time that was wasted on matters of little importance. Like George De Mestral, like my colleague at that high school reunion, like that schoolteacher, asking inquisitive questions can fill the world with new creations and it can forestall embarrassment, poor judgment, and aggravation.

Asking the right questions can help you score big in *Jeopardy*. It will also help you to score big in life.

---

1. Harold S. Kushner, *When Bad Things Happen to Good People* (New York: Schocken Books, 1981), pp. 136-138.

Coincidences

Scripture Lesson: John 10:11-18
   ... the good shepherd lays down his life for the sheep ...

Doctor Bernie Siegel claims that coincidences are God's way of remaining anonymous.

I have spent nine years here at the hospital. In the course of those nine years I've witnessed and experienced many strange things. I've watched events occur that made me stop and think and wonder. I've found myself doing something or I've found others doing something that made me scratch my head. I've come across many coincidences that made me wonder if indeed they were coincidences.

Probably the most common have centered on people who are dying. Families are called when their loved one slips into a coma and they literally camp out in the room, sitting and praying and holding hands, waiting for the moment of death to come. What happens often is that the family steps out of the room for a cup of coffee or just out in the hallway for a little air, and it is at that time when no one is around that the loved one dies. It is almost as though the person chose that moment so that he or she might spare the family the grief of witnessing the death.

I've also witnessed experiences of an opposite nature. A father was brought into the emergency room entering what would be the final stage of a very rapid illness. The father was given a room on the third floor and the son called on his brother to come home, explaining the gravity of the situation. The brother lived in Chicago. When I was called to the bedside 24 hours later, he was in a coma, his breaths were shallow. I suspected it would be a matter of minutes before his breathing would stop. I was wrong. He hung in for three more hours. He knew that the absent son was driving to the hospital from Chicago. Just as though he were waiting for him to get there, he took his last breath five minutes after that son arrived in the room.

A vivid memory from St. Ambrose, where I was last stationed, centered on one of the most beautiful men in the parish. His name was Paul Crowley. He worked many years for Mobil Refinery. He was the man in charge of the upkeep and the rebuilding of the parish boiler. Just as he was nearing retirement, he was stricken with cancer. He lived for three years following the diagnosis. At the end of the third year it became evident that it was a losing battle. Concerned very much for his wife's welfare, he wanted desperately to hang on long enough to qualify her for his pension. That would mean that he had to live up to a certain date. He fell into coma three days short of that date and then somehow managed to beat death until twenty minutes after midnight on the day when his wife would legally qualify for his retirement benefits.

Just last week, we had a patient in our hospice room who hung on till 2:00 a.m. the day of her fiftieth wedding anniversary.

In all these cases, those who were dying and in a coma, and allegedly unaware of anything happening around them, somehow managed to control the time of their death, holding it off so that a particularly loving goal might be reached. Surely, this does not happen all the time. There are countless examples of just the opposite happening, and the persons involved are just as loving and just as connected with their families as the ones I've mentioned. But the stories I have told do occur. The question is: Are we to write them off as a coincidence or is there a power at work here that supersedes our own?

Another incident that occurred at the hospital involved a different phenomenon. A woman called me, sounding very frantic. She wanted me to stop and see her husband because she had a terrible feeling that something had gone wrong. When I got to the husband's room, I was shocked to discover that he was dead. It must have happened just about the time that I received the call because the nurses reported that they had been in the room a few minutes earlier and at that time he was fine.

A friend of mine reported a true story of how a fishing boat was run down in the darkness of the night by an ocean liner.

Simultaneously, many miles away, the fisherman's wife awakened from a deep sleep with a loud shriek, calling out the name of her husband. She tried to go back to sleep but she found herself too agitated. In the morning she discovered that her husband had gone down with the boat right around the time she awakened from her sleep.

I hope this doesn't sound like a tabloid sermon. I hope you don't take this sermon to be an affirmation of the paranormal. I'm merely raising things that have happened which cause one to wonder if indeed they were coincidences or if, in fact, there's a power at work which supersedes our own.

Take a few cases that have marked the annals of history. On October 7, 1849, Edgar Allen Poe passed away, while on the same day James Whitcomb Riley, another American author and poet, was born. On October 9, 1845, a noted and prominent Catholic church leader, Redan, put off his clerical collar and left the church, while on that selfsame day John Henry Newman entered it. On February 12, 1809, Abraham Lincoln was born on one side of the Atlantic while Charles Darwin was born on the other side. On the same day in 1616, Shakespeare and Cervantes, two of history's most brilliant authors, passed away. On the day when a French mob tore the cross from Notre Dame and renounced Christianity, William Carey landed in India and claimed a new continent for Christ.

On July 4, 1826, the people of the United States were celebrating the Jubilee of the Declaration of Independence. Two of the great Independence presidents, John Adams and Thomas Jefferson, were still living. Adams was 91, Jefferson was 83. It was decided to make the Jubilee a festival in honor of the two veterans. From the Atlantic to the Pacific on the 4th of July, the names of Adams and Jefferson were toasted and acclaimed. The irony of it was that both died on that auspicious day. Adams passed away at sunset muttering,"Oh, well, Jefferson still lives." Unbeknown to him his old comrade had passed away several hours earlier. The Jubilee of Independence, the death of Adams, and the death of Jefferson all took place on the same day.

A boy's parents have left for a few hours and, in the absence of companions, he finds the time hanging heavily on his hands. He wanders into his father's library and pokes about among the books. He comes up with one that at least starts with a story. He suspects that there may be some philosophizing, sermonizing, or moralizing later on, but he tells himself that he can easily abandon it at that time. He scampers off to the loft in the stable next door, throws himself on the hay, and plunges into the book. He gets so captivated by the book that he can't put it down. He reads on and on and as he does, he feels the pull of the Holy Spirit. He's reading about people who have dedicated themselves to God and he gets the sense that he should do the same. At that moment, he falls upon his knees and, lifting up his heart and mind to God, he makes a decision to do what he has to do to pursue that goal.

That's one side of the story of Hudson Taylor, known as the apostle of the Chinese missions. The story has another side. When his mother returned, Taylor felt that he must confide to her what had just happened in the loft. But before he could even start the story, she interrupted him and told him that she already knew what he was going to say. Taken aback, Hudson Taylor asked how she could possibly know. The mother said that she had an hour to spare earlier in the afternoon, and she could think of nothing except him. So she decided to pray that he do something special with his life, that he go into the ministry. "What you're about to tell me," she said, "is that my prayers have been answered." On comparing notes, the two of them discovered that the hour the mother spent in prayer was the same hour the boy had spent in the loft.

This doesn't happen all the time. The stories occur only sporadically. They take place only every once in a while. And the truth is that a good majority of the time things go on that are not connected with any prayer or deadline. Deaths take place which fail to follow any script. People come and people go and there is no pattern or connection between their coming and their going, their birth or their death. The stories I've told are not a testimony for the paranormal gleaned from past issues of the *National Enquirer.* They are actual historical occurrences which have caused me to wonder whether they were mere coincidences or whether there is a higher power at work that supersedes our own.

Matthew Fox, the Dominican theologian, says that the moon is just the right distance from the earth for tides to happen. If the moon were just a little bit closer or a little bit farther, the tides wouldn't happen and thus the ocean would have been stagnant and thus no life could have emerged from the ocean. Fox said that the sun is not only the right distance from the earth, but there's also an ozone layer that lets in just the right amount of sunshine and keeps out just the right amount of radiation. If that weren't so, none of us would be healthy. Fox continues that the universe began as a large fireball some nineteen billion years ago. For 750,000 years the fireball expanded. We know now that if the fireball had expanded one millionth of a millionth of a millionth of a second faster or slower over those 750,000 years, you or I could not be here today. The earth would not have evolved in the way that it did. We also know that if the temperature of the fireball during those 750,000 years had been one degree colder or warmer, you or I would not be here today. Matthew Fox said we can call all that a coincidence or we can call all that the reality of God's unconditional and incredible love for us.

Jesus in our Gospel today alludes to the sheep and shepherd relationship of God and his people. In essence, he made it clear that God doesn't consider us trash but considers us special. God is not distant but near. The driving force of the universe is not hate but love. So maybe, just maybe, what passes for a coincidence might actually be a sample of the power of that love. Maybe, just maybe, what passes for a coincidence might actually be an example of God's loving touch in the running of the world. Perhaps Dr. Bernie Siegel had it right when he called coincidences God's way of remaining anonymous.

Recently, I was winding up the day and had just pushed the elevator button to take me to the second floor where my room had been located. I was going to change clothes and attend a party. As I got on the elevator, something made me think of a young man who was a patient whom I had seen the day before last. I knew this young man from a previous admission. As the door opened to the second floor, I decided not to get off and pushed instead the button for the floor on which the young man was located. When I entered the room, it was as though God had sent me. The young man asked to go to confession and proceeded to unleash a huge burden that he had carried for a long time. It was a deeply moving experience for both of us.

The irony was that he was going to be discharged in the morning and had I not stopped that night, the wonderful exchange of grace would have never taken place. Was it a coincidence that I thought of that young man at that time? Or was it the example of a power greater than my own? I'll put my money on the fact that it was God letting me know that the Shepherd was on the premises.

Calibrating Importance

Scripture Lesson: Mark 9:30-37
... they had argued with one another who was the greatest ...

A look into who or what is important.

Three young boys from a rather prestigious school were arguing as to whose father was the most important. The first boy said, "My dad is the ambassador to the United Nations, and when people see him they say, 'Your Excellency.'" The second boy said, "My dad is a prince, and when people see him, they say, 'Your Highness.'" The third boy said, "That's nothing. My dad weighs 450 pounds, and when people see him they say, 'O my God!'"

I've just humorously described one of many indicators that are used to measure importance. Society has established criteria for one to be designated as important and those indicators are derived from that criteria. The problem, however, is that it often misses the mark. All too often society leaves out of the criteria certain things that need to be taken into account when it comes to defining who is truly important.

Historian Howard Zinn talks about the fact that history does us a disservice because it tends to highlight headline-makers, and it fails to properly credit all the little people who, in essence, gave birth to the headlines.

For example, Abraham Lincoln is recognized as the one who ended slavery in this country. Although that may be so, if we look at the Emancipation Proclamation, the truth of the matter is that, prior to that proclamation, many people put their lives on the line to call attention to the evil of slavery. Many people were humiliated, harassed, and silenced because they dared attack an institution that provided considerable profit for many an influential person. Many a slave was killed because he dared to protest his indentured status. There would have been no Emancipation Proclamation if it were not for them and countless others who made no headlines, who received no credit, who will never make a history book, but who were vitally important in furthering the abolition of slavery.

The same can be said for all the other important causes, laws, and changes that have ended an evil or have promoted something that has helped create a better and more humane society. There will always be some person or persons who will be singled out as the most important, as the one who spearheaded the movement. But the truth of the matter is that they were no more important than were all the little people without whom there would be no movement.

A famous concert organist was giving a recital. It was back in the days before electricity, and the organ needed to be hand-pumped in order to produce sound. While the music was being played, there was a young fellow hidden behind the screen who pumped away with all the strength he had. During the intermission, the organist was standing in the wings and the young fellow, a small boy, came up to him and declared, "Aren't we great?" Rather sharply the organist retorted, "What do you mean, we?" The boy sheepishly went away. After the intermission, the organist sat down once again at the keys and not a sound came. He pressed again and still not a sound. Then the young boy poked his head around the screen and asked with a gleam in his eye, "Now, who's we?"

People may be recognized as important, of great worth, of great prestige, but they are no more important than all the little people, the boy or the girl, the man or the woman, who may not have pushed the pedals of the organ, but who somehow made it possible for them to rise to their prestigious position and carry out the work that they do.

Although society may measure importance by who is making the headlines, who is receiving the kudos and plaudits of the world at large, the reality is that countless others are as important and sometimes more important, although they are never recognized, they are never cited, and they never receive the acclaim they deserve.

Then there's the matter of being important, but not really standing for anything important. There is a true story about a man who parked his car in front of a supermarket. When he returned, he found the front of his car smashed and no sign of the offender's car. His heart sank until he noticed a scrap of paper tucked under the windshield wiper. Opening it he found this message: "As I'm writing this note to you, there are at least sixteen people watching me. They think I'm obviously giving you my name and address. Well, I'm not." The moral of the story is that very often the obvious is not the actual.

There are many people deemed important: professional football players, rock stars, entertainers, heads of state, movie stars, CEOs, bank presidents. Obviously they're important, but are they actually important? Are they doing anything that will have a long-term effect on the quality of life in the community in which they live? Are they doing anything as far as the state of the world is concerned? Will there be less poverty, less racism, less violence? Will they ever be remembered for having done something that has made this land of ours a better place in which to live? It seems to me that in computing one's importance we need to make a distinction between the obvious and the actual, between being important and doing important things. We have a lot of important people around today whom the generations that follow will find hardly important at all.

There are also those whose importance can't be denied but who have achieved their importance at the cost of their integrity. There's a great scene in the play and the movie *A Man for All Seasons*. Sir Thomas More is being tried for treason unjustly and illegally. One of the main witnesses testifying against him is an old protegé and a former friend. This man, Richard Rich, has agreed to lie about More's behavior and character and, in return, the King has made him the Prince of Wales.

As he walked past More sporting all the status symbols of his new regal position, Sir Thomas admonished his betrayer about the cost of his newfound importance. "For Wales?" he said. "Richard, it profits a man nothing to give his soul for the entire world, but for Wales?"

And how often has that been the case for people who have gained importance. They've clawed and scraped their way to the top. They've achieved the prestige, the status, they've always wanted. But it has come at the cost of their integrity; it has come at the cost of their humanity; it has come at the cost of their very soul.

Lee Atwater held a very important position. He was head of the Republican Party and was considered a campaign manager *par excellence*. He spearheaded the campaign that brought George Bush to the Presidency in 1989. He was diagnosed with brain cancer shortly afterwards. In the memoirs that he wrote shortly before he died, he made mention of the fact that he acquired more wealth, more power, more prestige than anyone could imagine. But with death staring him in the eye, he wished now that he had spent more time with his family. He wished now that he had spent more time with his friends. He wished that the time and energy he spent to achieve importance had been put toward those things that were really important.

When it comes to calibrating importance, we often tend to miscalculate. We designate certain people as important and we forget all the little people who are equally important if not more important than the ones getting the headlines. We designate certain people as important, but what qualifies them as important will never be judged or seen as such by the generations that follow ours. We designate certain people as important but we don't take into consideration the price they paid for their importance.

It is this whole question of calibration that Jesus addresses in today's Gospel. He catches the disciples arguing among themselves as to who is most important. In an effort to set them straight, he gathers them together and tells them that if anyone wishes to remain first he or she must remain the last one of all and the servant of all. In essence, he is telling them that, contrary to the way that society calibrates importance, if they really want to be important, they must give of themselves for the sake of others. They won't make headlines, they won't make millions, they won't command power, but their importance will go without question.

There is a story of a woman who had been used to every luxury and to immense respect. She had obviously achieved a great deal of status and importance. She died, and when she arrived in heaven an angel was sent to conduct her to her new home. They passed many a lovely mansion and the woman thought that each one must be the one allotted to her. When they passed through the main streets, they came to the outskirts where the houses were much smaller. At the very fringe, they came to a house that was little more than a shack. "This is your house," said the angel. "What!" said the woman. "That! I cannot live in that!" "I am sorry," said the angel, "but that is all we could build for you with the materials you sent up."

When all is said and done, it is not the status one receives in this world that matters. It is the status one receives in the next life that counts. It is not the materials we've accumulated here that are going to speak to our importance and our rank. The materials we send off to God and to the generations that follow will ultimately mark our importance. The mansions here do not matter. The mansions up there are the ones that count.

When we give of ourselves for the sake of others, when we do things that will be of service to humankind, when we put out so that others will enjoy a better life, we may not be deemed important by society but we'll live with the peace of mind that we've done good work. We'll live knowing that we haven't compromised our integrity or our soul just to be important. We'll live knowing that although people may not consider us as important as the rock star or the football player, at least we've done important things. We'll live with the satisfaction of knowing that, although someone else will get the credit for the grand noble deed, he couldn't have done it without our help.

When it comes to calibrating importance, follow the criteria of today's Gospel. Forego the mansion here for a place far greater in the world beyond this one.

Letter From God

Scripture Lesson: John 8:1-11

> *... Let anyone among you who is without*
> *sin be the first to throw a stone ...*

The Pharisees and the Scribes walked away acknowledging the fact that they were not without sin. I'm not too sure there are many today who would have done the same.

God called Saint Peter into the head office of heaven one day and told him they needed to get a count of everyone who would be coming to heaven in the next 100 years so they could make sure they had enough room. God instructed Saint Peter to go down to earth and take a door-to-door census. After only a few days on the job, it became obvious to Peter that it was too big a job to be handled alone. So he went back to God and suggested that instead of a door-to-door canvas they write a letter to everyone who would be coming to heaven in the next 100 years and do a census that way. God thought it was a good idea so they cranked up the Pearly Gates Printing Press, and they printed and mailed a letter to everyone who would be going to heaven in the next 100 years. And, of course, you all know what was in that letter!! (PAUSE) "YOU MEAN YOU DIDN'T GET ONE OF THOSE LETTERS?"

I was with a group of people when someone pulled that joke on us and I've been dying to use it ever since. I'm using it today because the fact of the matter is that if God were to send a letter to everyone alive today who will be going to heaven, a vast majority of us would truly expect to receive that letter. The *USA Weekend* magazine once conducted a poll and the data from the poll revealed that 75 percent of the respondents rated their chance of going to heaven as good to excellent. As a general rule, most of us believe that we're living in such a way that heaven will be our destiny.

It's nice to think that we're doing well when it comes to the conduct of our lives. Many of us are truly good and decent and loving people. But I'm just afraid that generally speaking we tend to overestimate our saintliness and underestimate our sinfulness. We tend to have many blind spots when it comes to an accounting of our lives.

Sir George Mellish was one of the great jurists of England. As a member of a committee appointed to draw up resolutions of congratulations for the Queen, he discovered that his colleagues had begun one resolution with the words: "Being conscious as we are of our own defects." "No! No!" said Judge Mellish. "That will never do. We cannot lie to her Majesty. Change it to: 'Being conscious as we are of one another's defects.'"

George Mellish was pointing out one of the many practices of ours that has kept us from honestly coming to grips with the reality of sin in our lives. As much as we'd like to think that we're fairly good when it comes to our conduct, as much as we'd like to think we're going to heaven, the fact of the matter is that quite often we're not as pure or as holy or as sinless as we think we are. Not only are we conscious of everyone else's defects and unconscious of our own, we are also good at other ways of blinding ourselves to all that is wrong in our life. We tend, for example, to rationalize our wrongs into rights.

Frederick II, an eighteenth century king of Prussia, went on an inspection tour of a Berlin prison. He was greeted with cries of prisoners who fell on their knees and protested their unjust imprisonment. While listening to these phony pleas of innocence, Frederick's eye was caught by a solitary figure in the corner, a prisoner seemingly unconcerned about all the commotion. "Why are you here?" Frederick asked him. "Armed robbery, your Majesty!" "Were you guilty?" the king asked. "Oh, yes, your Majesty, I entirely deserved my punishment." At that, Frederick summoned the jailer. "Jailer! Release this guilty man immediately. I will not have him kept where he will corrupt all the fine innocent people who occupy this prison."

We can chuckle at that story, but how often has it happened that we're guilty of a sin yet we claim our innocence, and that innocence rests on the fact that there was some sort of justification for our sin?

I was caught speeding once on Union Road at 1:30 a.m. The policeman had me doing 45 in a 30 mile-an-hour zone. I dutifully took the ticket, but I was upset. Here's a four-lane highway where nobody goes the speed limit, and they nail me. I went to the Cheektowaga Town Court to plead my case and my line of argument was that I was probably the slowest moving vehicle on Union Road that night. The DA said that was probably true, but he went on to say that it doesn't take away from the fact that I was speeding. What I was using was a line of logic that so often accompanies an accusation of wrongdoing. The fact that others were doing the same thing somehow made me innocent.

Along that same avenue of rationalization comes another way of claiming innocence — our ability to put a slant on our behavior that whitewashes what we would see as a sin in someone else. Zig Ziglar's book *Over the Top*[1] has a chapter listing a series of quips designed to indicate that very thing. Let me share a few of those quips:

> *When the other person blows up, he's nasty. When we do, it's righteous indignation.*
> *When she reads the riot act, she's vicious and insensitive; when we do it, we're just being honest for her own good.*
> *When we succeed we say, "Look what I did!" and when we fail we say, "Look what you made me do!"*
> *When she doesn't like your friends, she's prejudiced; when we don't like her friends, we're simply showing good judgment of human nature.*

Many things, which we would claim as sin if someone else did them, somehow become not sin when we do them. Many things which are obviously wrong, somehow become right when we do them.

A hillbilly gained a reputation for marksmanship. He could shoot a rifle with incredible accuracy. A man following him through the woods one day saw the evidence. On the trunk of a tree or on the side of a barn would be a round target drawn in chalk and there, dead center, would be a bullet hole. Finally the man caught up with the hillbilly and complimented him on his marksmanship. Then he asked him how he did it. "Oh, it's easy," said the hillbilly. "I just shoot the rifle and draw a circle around the bullet hole."

Often we do what we want to do. We do what we feel like doing, even though it's wrong. Then we get busy with words to prove how reasonable and understandable our behavior really is. We draw a circle of rationalization around the bullet hole.

As much as we'd like to think that we're pretty good when it comes to the conduct of our lives, as much as we'd like to think we're going to heaven, as much as we'd like to think that we're innocent of sin, maybe we would have second thoughts if we took note of how often we have rationalized our wrongs into rights. We might see how often we cleverly draw circles around our bullet holes, absolving ourselves from sin.

And if that weren't enough to give us second thoughts about receiving one of those letters from God, maybe we would think differently if we took note of how often we've blinded ourselves to our own sins by projecting them onto another.

I read this great story of a man who was perplexed by his wife's refusal to admit a hearing problem. Speaking with his doctor one day, he exclaimed, "How can I get my wife to admit she's hard of hearing?" "I'll tell you what you need to do," the doctor replied. "When you arrive home this evening, peek your head in the door and ask, 'Honey, what's for dinner?' If she doesn't answer, go into the living room and say, 'Honey, what's for dinner?' If she still doesn't hear you, then walk into the kitchen and ask, 'Honey, what's for dinner?' If she still does not answer, then walk up directly behind her and speak into her ear, 'Honey, what's for dinner?' Then you will convince her of her need for a hearing exam."

"Great!" the man responded, "I think it will work." That evening the man arrived from work. Just as he was instructed, he opened the front door and called out, "Honey, what's for dinner?" He listened carefully but there was no response. He walked into the living room and repeated, "Honey, what's for dinner?" He listened and still no answer. He then walked into the kitchen and asked, "Honey, what's for dinner?" Still, no answer. The man walked right up behind his wife and spoke directly in her ear, "Honey, what's for dinner?" At this point the wife turned around and sternly replied, "For the fourth time, I said we're having spaghetti."

So often when it comes to our own sin, we see it clearly in someone else yet we don't see it in ourselves. Psychologists call that projection. A good rule of thumb for checking on its practice is to analyze what it is that we find particularly despicable in the lives of the people we like or dislike. If we're honest and forthright in our analysis, we'll usually find that their sin happens to be our own. They're not hard of hearing; we are.

In today's Gospel, when the Scribes and Pharisees led a woman forward who had been caught in adultery, they quoted for Jesus the law which dictated stoning as the proper punishment. They asked for his comments, whereupon he simply bent down and started tracing on the ground with his finger. The scriptures don't tell us what he was tracing, but my guess is that he was tracing on the ground all the sins that the Scribes and Pharisees had either rationalized or projected away. Thus having exposed their less than perfect lives, thus having demonstrated the folly of their self-righteousness, Jesus uttered that famous line: "Let he who is without sin cast the first stone." With that they all dispersed, leaving the woman alone with Jesus.

There's nothing wrong with our believing that we're going to make it to heaven, that we're going to receive that letter from God; but perhaps we should give it a second thought. Maybe we'll discover, as George Mellish observed, that we're conscious of one another's defects but unconscious of our own. Maybe, like the man who followed that hillbilly in the woods, we'll discover that the reason we look so good is that we've drawn a circle of rationalization around the bullets of hate, vindictiveness, and rudeness that our rifles have fired. Maybe, like that man who went to see the doctor about his wife's hearing, we'll find that the sin we see in others is really the sin that's within ourselves.

You can go right on believing that heaven is your destiny, but don't be surprised if when you get to the pearly gates proclaiming a righteous life, Jesus starts tracing on the ground the sins you've cleverly and conveniently rationalized or projected away. It is better to be honest with yourself now and confess your sins than to continue with the illusion that somehow you're leading a life without sin. God longs to offer forgiveness. God longs to have you in heaven. Don't disappoint God. Face up to your sins before it's too late.

---

1. Zig Ziglar, *Over the Top* (Nashville: Thomas Nelson Publishers, 1994), p. 242.

One Day At A Time

Scripture Lesson: Mark 13:24-32
... but about that day or hour no one knows ...

The expression "one day at a time" is a favorite of twelve-step programs. Its wisdom goes without question.

If I were to ask you whether or not you can eat an elephant, most of you would say: "No!" "It can't be done!" "It's impossible!" "It's ridiculous even to consider it!" Yet the reality is that all of you can eat an elephant. Certainly not all at once, but if you ate small pieces over a long period of time, you could do it. You may not like it, but you could do it.

I'm beginning on a rather crazy note, proposing something preposterous, because the philosophy behind eating an elephant lies behind a cliché that has been a great help to a great number of people. It's the cliché "one day at a time." To those who are in the throes of a difficult problem or illness, to those who are facing something that seems overwhelming and impossible, one day at a time is the only way to go. One day at a time is the way it can be managed, handled, and overcome.

What I'd like to talk with you about today is living one day at a time. But not so much in deference to the down times of life, but more in terms of how that kind of living keeps us in touch with the wonder and beauty that is ever before us. Great experiences, golden opportunities, unbelievable and exhilarating moments in life often pass us by because we fail to live one day at a time.

An actor had had his day, but he wouldn't believe it. He used to go down to the theater in the morning when it was empty and go through all his popular roles again — the tragic, the comic — responding in play action to what he considered to be the breathless attention of the audience. But, of course, there was no audience, there was no curtain to bring down, and there was no applause

99

when the drama was over. The despair which he felt in his own soul was always echoed by the emptiness around him.

We all know people like that. Sometimes we're all a little like that ourselves. We live in yesterday instead of today. We keep looking to yesterday as though it were the only way that life could be lived, assigning to the past the sacredness and the purity that it never really had.

Samuel Johnson once said to an artist who wanted to paint his portrait that he wished to have his face painted "warts and all." Somehow, by a deft process, we remove the warts from the faces of the past, and we glorify it. We idealize circumstances and people and the possibilities that then existed, with little realization that if, by some miracle, we could live in the past, we wouldn't find it all that great, we wouldn't find it all that glorious. There's beauty, there's richness, there's wonder in the "one day of life" that is here right now. But if we choose to live in yesterday, it will all be missed and lost, and our lives will have been denied many wonderful experiences and blessings.

There are also those who are always living in tomorrow, who are letting the "one day at a time" slip through their fingers as they yearn for things yet to come. For example, a little girl is trying to be a young lady, a little boy can't wait to get out of school, a college student thinks of nothing except graduation. You might say to them, "Enjoy your youth! School days are the happiest days of your life!" But it all falls on deaf ears. A business person hangs on for the breakthrough product that will put him on easy street. A middle-aged factory worker lives for Saturday night to see if the lottery number she's chosen will match the ones on the television screen. A couple waits for the time when the mortgage will be paid. An elderly person counts off the days until retirement. In all these cases, the "one day at a time" is blurred because it is a future that they're waiting for. Life is put on hold until there comes that time when what they're waiting for has arrived.

I know a minister who is never in the church that he is in. He's always in the next one, the more prestigious one, the perfect one. So his present congregation receives only a fragment of his love and attention. His head and his heart are somewhere else. Already

100

he's deciding which church will be his new church and what he will do when he gets there.

One can visit a store which has the latest in electronic equipment, the state of the art in stereos, CDs, and cassettes. There will be many who will go there intent on buying something only to end up waiting for the price to be a little cheaper, the quality and texture of the product to be a little better. When the period of waiting is over, they may go there again only to hear a rumor of a whole new method of reproducing sound that will be coming out soon. They wait again. Then they come back and decide to hold out still longer for the real state-of-the-art stereo. All this time is going by when these persons are bereft of listening to any recorded music. The enjoyment of hearing a favorite musician gives way to traveling back and forth to the store.

One of the problems of living in tomorrow is that your life is always being held back. You're not enjoying today because you're waiting for that future time when everything will be right, when the perfect recording machinery can be bought, when the perfect job or church can be had, when all the loose ends of life can be neatly tied. And all the while, there's loveliness around you and under your feet, there's beautiful music being played and you're missing it all.

Living one day at a time carries with it a prescription: stop living in yesterday, stop living in tomorrow, and start living in today.

That, I believe, is the underlying theme of scripture texts traditionally presented in the lectionary during the final Sundays of the Church year. They deal with the end times, and the reality that we will never know the day or the hour when those end times will occur. The somewhat frightening message of Daniel in our first reading and of Jesus in our Gospel are meant to remind us that the tomorrow we're banking on isn't guaranteed, that things can happen which can rob us of our plans, our hopes, our dreams, and even our yesterdays.

One of the vintage *Twilight Zone* episodes back in the Rod Serling days centered on a short story that has become a classic in many literary circles. I'm referring to "The Occurrence at Owl Creek Bridge." It's the story of a man about to be hanged. Soldiers are leading him to a bridge that spanned a waterway called Owl Creek. In the center of the bridge, the man's hands and feet are tied and a rope, dropped from the top of the bridge, is put around his neck. When everything is ready, the commanding officer barks an order and the condemned man is pushed off the bridge, the rope securely tied to his neck and its end securely tied to the beam. Something strange happens. The rope breaks and the man goes plummeting to the creek far below. As he hits the water, he realizes that he's alive. He works hard to free himself from the rope around his hands, feet, and neck. Swimming quickly to the shore, he's ecstatic. He didn't die! He has a second chance at life! Suddenly, the world around him, all of the nature that circles the shore, takes on a beauty overlooked in the times prior to his walking on the bridge. The blueness of the sky, the arching branches of the trees, the shape of the leaves, the wild flowers, fill him with ecstasy. They've never looked so wonderful. Then a bullet zings through the air and off he runs into the woods. He runs and runs, and soon he sees a house with a white fence around it. As the gate opens, he can't believe his eyes. He's back home again. He then sees his wife running from the front door to meet him. He can't wait to embrace her. Just as he's inches short of this wonderful exchange of love, the camera jarringly takes us back to Owl Creek Bridge. The man who was about to embrace his wife is seen dangling from the bridge, a rope tied around his neck.

The apparent new lease on life had never occurred. It was just something he imagined as he was pushed off the bridge. With death staring him in the eye, the beauty of nature and the love of his wife took on a richer, deeper dimension, spawning a most wonderful dream. But, unfortunately for him, it was just a dream. It was too late to appreciate and relish what was once real.

That is the payoff for living one day at a time. One can come to know and appreciate life before it's too late, before something happens that can make the beautiful things of life only a fleeting dream. Death has robbed too many people of the tomorrow that they longed for, the time they were banking on to enjoy life. Because we never know the day nor the hour of our death or of some illness, it is imperative that we live in the present, that we live for today, that we take life one day at a time.

Dr. Frank Boreham was a distinguished Australian preacher and author. One weekend he was a guest preacher in a distant church, and he stayed overnight in the home of one of the members. Coming downstairs in the morning, he noticed that in the clear glass of the window on the landing were the scriptural words: "This is the day the Lord has made, let us be glad and rejoice in it!" At breakfast, he mentioned the unusual window to his hostess, and he found her eager to explain it. She said there was a period in her life when remembrances of the past were paralyzing and the thought of the future terrifying. One day, her eyes fell upon the words of the psalmist: "This is the day the Lord has made, let us be glad and rejoice in it!" She came to realize that she had to live one day at a time. When she did so, the past wasn't so paralyzing, the future wasn't so terrifying. She began to notice the beauty around her, the joy that was available to her. So she had the word of the psalmist carved into the window so that she would remind herself every morning of the need to discover the wonder and the excitement of the day that was unfolding before her.

The scripture reading of today and those of next week remind us that life is short and that we never know the day nor the hour when we might find ourselves atop some Owl Creek Bridge with the beauty of life and nature being some fleeting dream. It is imperative that we not put off things that are important, that we not postpone to a future date something joyful and enriching, that we not wait too long to do the things we've longed to do. It is imperative that we live for today and not for tomorrow or yesterday. "This is the day the Lord the Lord has made, let us be glad and rejoice in it!"

There's an old story of a sailing ship that was crippled off the coast of South America. Sighting a friendly vessel, it sent up the signal: "Water, water, we die of thirst." The answer came back: "Cast your bucket where you are!" The captain of the distressed vehicle thought there must be a mistake. So he repeated the signal and received the same answer. He didn't know that they were just then crossing the Amazon ocean current and that instead of being in salt water, they were actually sailing in fresh water. Finally, he did what he was told, cast down his bucket, and it came up with fresh, sparkling water from the mouth of the Amazon River.

Wherever we are right now, in whatever season we are living, God has surrounded us with opportunities, challenges, resources, beauty, and wonder that we have never seen before and may never see again. So the way of wisdom is not to live in the past or live in the future, but to cast down our buckets where we are.

My friends, live one day at a time. Remember: "This is the day the day that the Lord has made, let us be glad and rejoice in it."

Calling A Spade A Spade

Scripture Lesson: John 20:19-31
   ... Unless I see ... I will not believe ...

I must credit the Reverend R. Maurice Boyd for this talk. Many of its ideas stemmed from "Consequences of Candor," a chapter in his book *Corridors of Light.*[1]

Back in my seminary days, good teachers were hard to come by. You tended to cherish those few who knew their craft well and actually excited you into learning. One of those stellar teachers was a gentleman by the name of Bruce Hammond. Our class was the very first one he taught when he came on as an adjunct professor from Canisius College. He was the Director of Communications there and the authorities at the seminary thought he would make a good first year homiletics teacher. He didn't make a good teacher, he made a great one. He was particularly great at critiquing the homilies, pointing out the flaws and the weaknesses and explaining why it may have been ineffective had it been preached on a Sunday morning. What made the critiquing effective was Dr. Hammond's candor. As the Irish would say, he "called a spade a spade." He didn't pull any punches. He wasn't afraid to be brutally frank and honest. Although that might mean a ruffled feather or two, it helped make the guys better preachers, and it helped them realize that they were far from perfect when it came to delivering homilies. Two years later, I learned he was about to be let go by the seminary. It turned out that too many of the students complained about him. In essence, they couldn't handle his candor; they couldn't take his frank opinions about their preaching.

I was sad to hear that and sadder still that student opinion bore so much power. I raise up the Bruce Hammond story because I would like to talk with you today about candor and frankness. As evidenced by my opening remarks, they are often two-edged swords. They are virtues which are welcomed and applauded by

105

some and at the same time rejected and scorned by others. They are seen as honorable and noble by some while at the same time despicable and boorish by others. Candor and frankness are seen as assets by some and liabilities by others, useful and helpful by some and destructive and malicious by others. There is no getting around the fact that they happen to have Jekyll and Hyde characteristics. The heralds and the detractors of the virtues are both correct in their assessments. Candor and frankness can be harmful, and they can be helpful. Let's consider the positive and the negative.

A math teacher always ended his presentation of a lesson with the question, "Is that clear to you or should I go over it again?" For most of us, it was about as clear as mud but hardly anyone had the guts to say so. But, thank God, there was someone in the class who had the candor to speak up, who wasn't afraid to admit frankly that he didn't know or understand what the teacher was talking about. We loved him for his candor and frankness, because it meant that we, who were equally ignorant, were able to keep our ignorance anonymous and at the same time cash in on a clearer presentation of a lesson we didn't understand.

That's one of the positive things about candor. It makes for clarity; it helps eliminate confusion. It's just too bad that most of us are like we were in the classroom — afraid to open our mouths, afraid to admit frankly that there's something we don't understand.

I know of many patients who are either too timid or too polite to speak up to their doctors. Unfortunately, as a result, they end up misunderstanding what he or she had to say. In my role as chaplain, I often serve as an interpreter for doctors, and I'm convinced that had the patients confessed their confusion to the doctor, they wouldn't have needed me to sort out the facts. They would have felt greatly relieved a lot earlier knowing more clearly where they stood when it came to their diagnosis.

Each year I make an annual trip to the Chautauqua Institution and invariably when I'm in the outdoor amphitheater a speaker will come along who will not make proper use of the microphone. Whenever that happens, you can always bank on the fact that a group of Chautauquans will shout out, "I can't hear you!" Whenever that happens, my colleague, Father Jim Croglio, complains about their behavior, citing it as an act of rudeness. I always counter his complaint, defending those Chautauquans. What's usually true is that he and I had a hard time hearing as well. If those so called "rude Chautauquans" didn't speak up, a majority of us would have missed the talk. So I level with him and ask whether he'd like us all to be polite and quiet and thus not hear the speaker or to be frank and outspoken and, thus, cajole the speaker into using the microphone properly, allowing us all to hear what he or she had to say.

It makes absolutely no sense to sit in confusion, to miss hearing a wonderful speaker, to miss understanding something very important, to be left in the dark on matters of grave significance when all it takes is a little candor to clear the air, to improve the situation, to repair a misunderstanding, or to eliminate a confusion.

Another positive about frankness and candor is that it helps improve one's talents and abilities. Not everyone is like the seminarians who complained about Doctor Hammond. Many people appreciate someone's speaking with candor because it helps alert them to a flaw or bad habit that may have escaped their attention.

Whenever comedian Jay Leno receives a negative note about his comedy, he calls the author so that he might learn what it was he said that turned out to be upsetting. He also drives to certain comedy clubs near his home where he knows that the audiences pull no punches and openly comment about the quality of his work. In that way, he knows just what he has to do to improve his act.

I think Jay Leno typifies a great number of talented people. Candor and frankness on the part of others prove extremely helpful because they lead to the honing, the developing, the improving of their talents and abilities. Admittedly, it isn't easy hearing someone make negative comments about how we do our jobs, but credit those who do so with the candor to speak up, and then use the criticism to your own advantage.

Anthony De Mello in one of his books[2] has this great two-liner:

> *A monkey on a tree hurled a coconut at the head of the master. The man picked it up, drank the milk, ate the flesh, and made a bowl from the shell.*

The line at the bottom read: "Thank you for your criticism of me."

Candor has the ability to expose fraud and deception, especially in regard to our behavior. It often lays open the illusion of innocence and decency.

I think we're all familiar with that scripture passage which centers on Jesus and the adulterous woman. As you might remember, just as she was about to be stoned, Jesus kneels down and begins writing in the sand. A moment or two later everyone drops his stone and walks away. Now the Gospel never comes out and says what Jesus was writing in the sand, but many scholars will claim that Jesus was merely writing down all the sins of the people who were about to hurl the stones. He was confronting them with the fact that contrary to what was probably their own understanding about themselves, they were far from lily white. They were hardly more upright than the very woman they were about to stone.

James Burtchaell, the Holy Ghost Friar, produced a tape[3] regarding confession. In it he points out that our most grievous sins are the ones that have eluded our conscience. They are the ones we hardly realize we commit. It's only through a friend's candor and our willingness to accept that candor that we come to the realization that there are certain things we do that are less than noble, less than honorable, less than decent, less than kind.

Gogol wrote a play in which he revealed the emptiness of our pretension and the foolishness of our hypocrisy. He mocks both, and he has the audience laughing hysterically at those who are characterizing that pretension and that hypocrisy. But suddenly in the midst of the play, one of the characters faces the audience and asks who it is they're laughing at. He goes on to answer his own question. They're laughing at themselves, for nothing is revealed on stage that is not present in the hearts of the audience. In a matter of minutes, the laughter comes to an abrupt end.

We all need friends who can do for us what that character from Gogol's play did for his audience — friends who tell us not what we want to hear but what we should hear, friends who puncture through our denial and with great candor reveal aspects of our life that need changing. We need friends who won't be part of the conspiracy of silence that allows our sins to destroy us as well as those we love.

Candor and frankness can thus perform many valuable services. The virtues can insure clarity; they can prevent misunderstanding; they can help develop talent and ability; they can expose fraud and deception.

But then, of course, there's the other side. Frankness and candor can also inflict harm. If used unwisely and cruelly, they can impose undue pain and suffering.

We had a discussion at our last bio-ethics committee meeting about truth-telling in medicine. Two points were made. If, with great frankness and candor, one tells a pre-surgical patient all that can go wrong in surgery no matter how minuscule a possibility, so much fear can be injected in the patient that he or she will enter surgery with a negative mental attitude that can be detrimental to survival. Second: If, with great candor and frankness, one spells out for a post-surgical patient the entire ten yards of the prognosis, one risks the possibility of destroying his or her hope and hastening death via a self-fulfilling prophecy. We were all in agreement that the truth must be told, but we all agreed that one must exercise some precaution when it comes to candor and frankness. An overload of the two virtues can sometimes prove detrimental to health.

Candor and frankness must be tempered by wisdom and understanding. They must always be tempered by compassion and kindness. Many brilliant people exercise candor and frankness, but they do so out of spite and arrogance as they rip apart those less gifted than themselves. Many prejudiced people exercise candor, but they do so with venom in their veins as they openly castigate a particular race of people. Many mean-spirited people have a reputation for being very frank, and their virtue degrades and diminishes other human beings. Candor and frankness are wonderful virtues, but if they are not exercised with wisdom, compassion, and love, they can be instruments of pain, suffering, and cruelty.

Every octave of Easter, the main character in the Gospel is Thomas. He's been famous as the doubter, but the reality is that it's a bum rap. He was no more skeptical or doubtful than were the other disciples. What really distinguished him was that he was more direct than the rest of the twelve. What he felt, he said. What he saw, he declared. He called a spade a spade. He was not afraid to speak his mind. He was the premier exhibitor of the virtues of frankness and candor, and Jesus loved him for it; he honored those virtues.

On this octave of Easter, let us pray that we might be courageous enough to exhibit frankness and candor where it is needed, doing so always with wisdom and with compassion. If there is a misunderstanding, if something needs to be clarified, if there is something foolish occurring, if we see something that is bothering us, if we notice a friend steering down a wrong path, may we not hesitate to speak. And if there happens to be a Dr. Bruce Hammond type pointing out flaws and exposing our sin, may we never think of disowning that person. May we never write off what he or she has to say about our behavior and talent. Be a Saint Thomas in the world you're living in and embrace Saint Thomas when he comes your way.

---

1. R. Maurice Boyd, *Corridors of Light* (Hamilton, Ontario: Colonsay House, 1991), pp. 95-105.

2. Anthony De Mello, *The Song of the Bird* (Garden City, N.Y.: Image Books, 1982), p. 163.

3. James T. Burtchaell, *Bread & Salt: A Catholic Catechism* (NCR Credence cassettes, 1982), Forgiveness.

What About Us Grils?

Scripture Lesson: Matthew 2:1-12
... wise men from the East came ...

I credit the late Dr. Bruce W. Thielemann for the image of the "gril." This is an attempt to console and affirm the "grils" who are often pained by their exclusion from the mainstream of life.

On a wall of a subway station in New York City was an advertising poster that depicted a very dignified elderly gentleman recommending a particular product. And someone, probably a little boy, wanted to deface the advertising and drew a kind of balloon coming out of the mouth of the dignified elderly gentleman. And then this youngster wrote in the balloon the dirtiest thing he could think of to say. He wrote "I like" and he meant to write girls, but he made a mistake. Instead of writing girls, g-i-r-l-s, he wrote grils, g-r-i-l-s. "I like grils." Someone had come along and with a felt-tipped pen had written under that, "It's girls, stupid, not grils." Then another party, for the handwriting was still different, had come and written under that: "But then, what about us grils?" *What about us grils?*

There is no definition for grils contained within a dictionary, but I believe grils exist. Grils happen to be those people that nobody seems to like, those people who feel they've been crowded out of the middle of life, pushed aside, shoved somewhere where they're made to feel alone and unwanted. Grils are the fifth-wheel people who don't seem to fit anymore in the mainstream of life, people whom no one seems too happy or too comfortable having around.

It's the person who is suddenly diagnosed with a life-threatening disease, maybe the dreaded AIDS virus. Although shown all the support and encouragement in the world in the early days of the diagnosis, in time it seems as though people drift away. They don't know what to say to someone who is sick, so they don't bother coming around anymore. Furthermore, those old friends are engaged

111

in strenuous activities that are beyond the range of acceptable behavior for someone who's sick. In a short time, the person with a life-threatening disease begins to feel as though he or she has been abandoned. One begins feeling like a gril.

Then there are the recently widowed or divorced. They were used to going out with other couples. They had a lot of fun going to various night spots, going to house parties, bowling in a mixed couples league. But now, because they don't have a spouse, there's a sense of awkwardness, there's a sense of not fitting in anymore. Phone calls and invitations drop off. One begins feeling like a gril.

There are the people who are fat and know people are looking at their fat and talking about their fat. There are the people who are homely, who are not very physically endowed and who sense laughter whenever their backs are turned. There are those who haven't been taught social graces and come across as sloppy because their clothes don't match and their hair never seems combed. There's that guy or gal who has two left feet, who can't seem to keep food on the plate or drink in a glass. These types of people often feel left out, out of sync with the rest of the world. They're grils of the first degree.

And how about the teenage boy or girl who happens to excel in school, or anyone for that matter who achieves any degree of success? Envy and resentment have ways of isolating them from the pack. They're often led to believe that they're grils.

Take the young boy or girl who resists peer pressure, who says "no" to drugs and "no" to sex, who says "no" to joining a gang, "no" to wearing the latest in fashions, who speaks out against prejudice and bigotry and gossip. We applaud them for it. But it often carries the price of being made into a gril, being made to feel that they lie outside the mainstream of school life.

And what about that person who has made a mistake, who has done something wrong, violated some law? It has made the newspaper. It has become the hottest item of conversation amongst friends. That person feels one inch tall, and, in quick fashion, he or she is *persona non grata*, an unwelcome guest in any company, a gril.

Needless to say, grils are in great numbers. They make up various castes of people. They are the boys and girls, the men and women, who do not feel welcome, who don't seem to fit in, who feel left out of the mainstream of life. They are those who are made to believe that they are fish out of water, square pegs in round holes.

It is to people such as these that the feast of the Epiphany speaks. It is the celebration of a God who happens to like strange people, a God who runs a club that isn't particular as to its members, a God who has a Son who is not ashamed of the company he happens to keep.

When we recollect the manger scene, we have a way of glamorizing everything about it. In our imagination, we deem the shepherds as clean, honest, and fairly religious fellows. In reality, they were unclean and ignorant, the social outcasts of their day. As for the Wise Men whom we particularly recollect on this day, we think of them as oil-rich sheiks or university-educated Hindus. Some in history have even gone so far as to call them kings. The reality was far from that. They were merely foreigners, Scripture calls them astrologers, and they were as far from the mainstream of life as were those shepherds.

The very first to be welcomed by Christ were, in essence, grils. They were people who felt left out of the society in which they lived. The manger scene was the first in a series of countless messages to grils throughout the world, the message that in God's kingdom, grils are welcome. They're special. They are loved.

A statue of Christ was carved by Bertel Thorwaldsen, the great Danish sculptor. It was commissioned by the King of Denmark some 100 years ago. It was to portray Christ as a powerful and strong king. So Thorwaldsen molded a tall Christ with shoulders thrown back, head erect, and arms extended in power. Just before applying the finishing touch, Thorwaldsen was called out of town. While absent, the sea mist that often pervades Denmark filtered into his studio and caused the statue to melt so much so that the arms that were extended were now hanging limply. The head that was erect was now bent low. The shoulders that had been thrown back were now drooping. When Thorwaldsen returned and saw what happened, he considered the statue ruined. But as he gazed upon its sorrowed state, it came to him that the image that was now before him was more representative of Christ than was the strong and powerful figure he had originally sculpted. Instead of restructuring the drooping image of Jesus, he merely took his carving tool and carved at the bottom the words: "Come to me all you who labor and are heavy burdened and I will give you rest."

To anyone who has a life-threatening disease, to anyone who feels overwhelmed and crestfallen by the trials and tribulations of life, to anyone in pain whose life is filled with sorrow and suffering and loneliness, to all you grils, that melted statue speaks to you. That melted statue captures the essence of God made man in Jesus Christ. For his whole life, especially his crucified self, was a testimony of his desire to be identified with you. It was a testimony of his desire to embrace you and claim you as his own. Just as Baby Jesus was welcoming to the grils of the manger scene, the adult Jesus was welcoming to the grils of the Jerusalem scene and the Jericho scene and the Calvary scene, and all the places where the sick, the lame, the poor, and the lonely abound.

I was a bit miffed recently when I read a small piece in the *National Catholic Reporter* which mentioned that a particular group of Catholics was petitioning Rome to reinstate excommunication. In particular, they wanted Rome to banish people like Mario Cuomo and Ted Kennedy from the Church. I may not be particularly happy with Catholic public figures who are wishy-washy on abortion, but I always thought that the Church stood for forgiveness and love, not for harshness and severity. Unless I'm reading it wrong, I don't remember Jesus condemning sinners; I only remember his embracing sinners. Unless I'm selecting only the softer parables, I thought that most centered on the theme of forgiveness. The parable of the lost coin, the lost sheep, and the prodigal son, to name just a few, all point to a God with arms open for each and every sinner.

There's a very beautiful old legend which pictures the end time, the day of the Lord that the Scriptures foretold. In paradise on the last day, everyone is celebrating, dancing, and singing with great jubilation, everyone, that is, except Jesus. Jesus is standing very quietly in the shadows of the gates of paradise. Somebody asks him what he is doing and why he is not celebrating. He says, in reply, "I'm standing here waiting for Judas. I won't be happy until

114

he comes home." That legend repeats the story of the parables. That legend speaks of the loving, forgiving spirit that Jesus described as inhabiting the kingdom of God.

To all you grils out there who are weighed down by some mistake you've made, some sin you've committed, some awful embarrassing thing you've done, God says, "Come home! All is forgiven! I can't wait to welcome you!"

A shepherd was out one night in the woods. He was looking for some sticks to help stoke a fire. As he walked about on this moonless night, he suddenly encountered someone hiding in the rocks. He said, "Friend, do not hide from me. Come and join me by the fire and get warm." And the outcast replied, "You would not want me to come to your fire." "Oh, yes, I would," said the shepherd, "I would be delighted to have you there no matter who you are." With that he picked up some sticks and started back to the place where the fire had already begun and he placed them on the fire. As it burned brighter, the outcast who had followed came into the light. It revealed a face that was hideously disfigured with leprosy. And the shepherd, looking at him, smiled and said, "Come around to this side of the fire by me. It is warmer here and there is less smoke." The leper paused for a moment and came around. He smiled and it was an ugly smile but it was the first smile he had known in years.

That story captures yet another aspect of the manger message. The leper didn't have to ask to come to the fire, he was invited. And so it is with all who feel like lepers, who feel as though they're ugly because they're fat, they're homely, they're awkward, they're different. God doesn't care what you look like. The invitation is there for you to join his family. You may think you're a gril, but it doesn't matter to God. His fire is burning and he wishes you to join him by the fire.

A legend says that Hasad, a righteous person, went to Sodom and Gomorrah to speak out against the injustice, the cruelty, the bigotry that was prevalent in those cities. Week after week, month after month, he continued to speak his message of righteousness, but it fell on deaf ears. No one listened. Finally, a young man came up to him and said, "Why do you bother speaking out? No one is listening to you." And Hasad said, " When I first began to speak out I really believed I could change the people of Sodom and Gomorrah. Now I know that I must continue to speak out so that the people of Sodom and Gomorrah don't change me."

To those of you feeling ostracized because you speak out against racial prejudice, sexual dishonesty, and wrongful priorities; to those of you feeling left out because you use your talents and gifts while so many around you don't; to those of you feeling alone because you've decided to resist the pressure of your peers to do something you know is wrong, don't lose heart! Don't let the crowds change you! Realize that you have an ally in Jesus who often found himself running counter to the culture, the morals, and the habits of his time and day. Realize that Jesus was a gril just like you.

The feast of the Epiphany which we celebrate today was the beginning of a message of acceptance and love for all the grils of the world, for all those feeling crowded out of the mainstream of life. By welcoming and embracing such gril types as the shepherds and the astrologers, the tone was set for God's kingdom.

To those of you who feel lonely and forgotten because you're ill or you're alone or you're hurting, God says, "Come to me all you who labor and are heavy burdened and I will give you rest." To those of you who have done something wrong and feel isolated as a result, God says, "Come home, all is forgiven." To those of you who feel as though you're ugly or you're awkward or you're different, God says: "Come join me by the fire so I can see your lovely face." To those of you feeling alone because you're the only one speaking out for virtue, honesty, and truth, God says, "I know how you feel. You're my ally." To all you grils, God loves you! God cares for you! God has a special place in his heart for you!

Is It Real Or Is It Memorex?

Scripture Lesson: Matthew 13:24-30
  ... When the plants came up and bore grain,
    then the weeds appeared as well ...

When the counterfeit passes for the real, problems ensue.

Charlie Chaplin was one of the truly great stars of the silent screen. In those days, when his name occupied the marquees of movie theaters everywhere, he was probably the most popular man alive. People stood in lines for hours to get into his films, even in the rain and snow. It was not uncommon to find almost everyone impersonating some of the Chaplin characteristics that made him such a success. The funny strut, the short steps, the twirled umbrella were imitated by thousands of fans.

It got to the point where county fairs had contests for impersonations of Charlie Chaplin. The real Chaplin was traveling in the Eastern United States when he saw in front of him a poster advertising such a Chaplin impersonation competition. The prize was $100. He entered the contest. When his turn came, he sauntered onto the stage with his black bowler hat, his baggy pants, the rolled umbrella, and the funny toothbrush moustache. He didn't inform anyone that he was the *bona fide* Charlie Chaplin. Fifteen others appeared on stage doing their best impersonation. When the judges tallied the votes, the real Chaplin finished eleventh. Ten make-believe Charlie Chaplins were chosen over the real thing.

It's interesting to note how easily people can be fooled by imitations. What happened at that county fair is not highly unusual. People all too often cannot distinguish the real thing from the counterfeit. People all too often can be led astray by that which is anything but genuine.

A recent controversy involves pop singer Madonna. She has been accused of not really singing her songs during her concerts. Supposedly she merely mouths the words while the public address

117

system puts on her recorded voice. Concert attenders are thus not really hearing a live concert but a recorded concert. Although Madonna refuses to comment on the charges, it has come to be known that many performers operate in just such a counterfeit way. Groups like Bon Jovi and New Kids on the Block are just two examples; they regularly faked the singing of their songs in concerts. It is interesting that no one knew that until now. Counterfeit performances have been going on and literally millions were none the wiser. Millions actually thought they were hearing the genuine live voices of their favorite musical group. It is only now that they have come to realize they have been deceived.

So we find that many can be led to mistake the counterfeit for the real, that many can be fooled into believing something is genuine when in fact it really isn't. As much as we pride ourselves in being very perceptive people, we are prone to deception. We can be taken in by that which is a fake; we can be fooled by people whom we thought to be the real thing.

I remember once mobilizing my old parish to help a young man who had just arrived in the neighborhood. He had a young bride and a young child and he needed some provisions; he needed some help to get started. I got the St. Vincent de Paul Society to give the family some vouchers for food. Mentioning his plight to some parishioners, they came up with an old refrigerator for his apartment. Some donated diapers; some provided dishes, pots, and pans. There was an impressive outpouring of help from every corner for these young people who had just moved into the parish.

Shortly after this neighborhood-wide mobilization, it was discovered that this young man was a fugitive from the law. He had been charged with armed robbery in Rochester. It was revealed that his wife wasn't really his wife — that she was a teenage girlfriend who had been reported missing by her family and the subject of a nationwide search. At least the child was legitimately theirs. When the real story behind this "hard luck couple" became known, they disappeared.

Everything this parish and I did were done in good faith, but it was particularly unnerving that none of us was perceptive enough to recognize the lie. None of us caught on to the holes in their fabricated story. It especially bothered me because I thought I was an expert at reading people.

Even though we think we can't be fooled, we often are. There really are no exceptions when it comes to being duped by a counterfeit. It is highly doubtful that we would have fared much better had we been one of those judges at the county fair where the real Charlie Chaplin mixed himself in with his impersonators.

Because we often cannot distinguish what is genuine from what isn't, because we often cannot tell what is real from what is counterfeit, we end up securing an attitude based on someone or something that is phony. We tend to become jaded because we have been duped by a counterfeit. We let our feelings about a fraud become our feelings about the real thing.

I have to confess that ever since I was taken in by that "hard luck couple" who came to me for help I've grown suspicious of anyone who approaches me in a similar fashion. I tend now to doubt the veracity of many of the hard-luck stories I hear. I now, periodically, hold back my compassion and my empathy — all because of that counterfeit couple who crossed my path.

Isn't this often the way prejudices are formed? Isn't that the way we view so many things in life? We learn of a family on welfare who makes more money than we do and who happens to be driving a Cadillac. Right away, everyone on welfare becomes suspect. They are judged by that one fraudulent family. We encounter a person of a particular ethnic background who happens to typify less than admirable qualities and right away a whole nationality gets painted with the same brush. An opinion is formed based on a counterfeit.

One of the saddest stories that I often hear revolves around elderly people who will tell of a negative experience they had in confession many years ago. They went to a priest who hollered at them, a priest who belittled them. Because a priest was anything but the merciful and compassionate Christ he was supposed to be, they haven't been to church or confession since. Their experience with a counterfeit left an indelible mark. Their brush with someone who was not a genuine priest implanted an attitude that was hard to unearth.

That is usually the biggest problem with counterfeits — they tend to leave the most lasting of memories and the deepest impression.

A colleague of mine, Bruce Thieleman, a Presbyterian pastor, once made reference to that reality by envisioning the discovery of a counterfeit ten-dollar bill in a bank. He said, "You can just imagine how every single teller will examine and look at the bill. It will be the talk of the bank for an entire day. Meanwhile, tens of thousands of genuine ten-dollar bills will pass through people's hands with hardly a cursory glance, with hardly a comment."

We must always be on guard that we don't let an encounter with a fraud leave us jaded and cynical. We must never allow the counterfeit to rule our lives or our attitudes or our point of view.

Today's Gospel tells us the famous story of the wheat and the weeds. The weed that Jesus was describing was the bane of the farmer's existence in Jesus' day. It was called a darnel and its growing habits were such that it was virtually indistinguishable from the wheat. Its leaves, height, color — all its outward characteristics — were identical. Only when the fruiting heads began to appear could one tell them apart.

God was trying to tell us through that parable that there are plenty of counterfeit look-alikes in the world, that what passes for wheat could very well be a weed. We can be fooled very easily no matter how perceptive we think we might be. Since the world is constructed in such a manner, it's extremely important that we don't condemn an entire patch of wheat just because the particular shoots we picked turned out to be weeds. It is imperative that we not condemn an entire generation, an entire profession, an entire gender, an entire nationality, an entire race just because we happen to encounter one of their counterfeits. It is imperative that we not pass judgment or form attitudes just because we have been fooled by that which is other than genuine.

We are all familiar with the Raggedy Ann doll. The floppy, loose-limbed rag doll with the silly grin and the colorful outfit still wins the day for most young children. A few years ago a minor scandal took place. Counterfeit Raggedy Ann dolls hit the market. People were duped into buying what was not the real thing. The only way it was possible to tell the real doll from the counterfeit was to look underneath the silly clothing. On the chest of every real Raggedy Ann doll is a painted heart with a tiny printed message that reads, "I love you." One could only tell the real doll by going beneath the surface to find the heart.

Those judges at that county fair might have been able to spot the genuine Charlie Chaplin had they looked deeper than just at the external appearance. If we are bruised and jaded because of some encounter with a counterfeit, the best cure is a probe beneath the surface the next time we meet someone of a particular gender or nationality or race or profession who hurt us. We may find the one with the painted heart that reads, "I love you!" We might be cured of the prejudice we hold.

18-Inch Gap

Scripture Lesson: Mark 12:28-34
... love the Lord your God with all your heart, and with all your soul, and with all your mind, and with all your strength ...

In an interesting twist, the talk was well received by some patients, not so much because of the point, but because my opening comments helped alleviate fears in regard to their bizarre mental behavior. They hadn't realized that what they experienced was not far from the "norm" when it comes to surgery.

Several years ago, we had a celebrity patient here at Sisters Hospital whose name will go unmentioned. He was here for surgery. It went well and he was placed in one of our step-down intensive care units. Later that night, he ran into all kinds of problems, none of them medical. The person in question began to hallucinate and we had an awful time trying to convince him that things were different from the way he saw them.

That's not, I'm afraid, an all too uncommon post-surgical experience. Every once in a while the drugs used for pain control or some other surgically-related problem wreak havoc with people's minds and they begin to think they're somewhere else. Their bodies are in a hospital bed, but their minds are back at home sitting at a desk or lying on the bed, carrying out some chores. Thank God it is just a temporary problem. Once the drugs in question are out of their system, they're back to normal with hardly a recollection of their strange behavior.

When you come right down to it, we've all had that kind of experience. No, I'm not referring to how we might have behaved following a surgical procedure. I'm not talking about having hallucinations, I'm talking about the experience of being somewhere physically and being somewhere else mentally. Call it daydreaming or a lack of concentration, we've all had the experience of having our minds drift off to another place while our bodies were secured at a meeting or at a function or in a church pew or in the midst of some routine activity.

The disconnection of mind from body is often at the heart of many a problem. The reason we might be sick, the reason we might be unhappy, the reason we weren't able to accomplish something, the reason we're feeling empty inside can often be traced to that disconnection. When the mind is not in sync with the body, when they're going in two different directions, many negative things occur and many positive things fail to happen. The same holds true when we factor in the heart and soul as well.

The ancient Greeks used to set up in the middle of their cities centers which they called *asplexia*. Under one roof was housed a gymnasium for the well, a hospital for the sick, and a temple to serve both. It proved to be a treatment center for the body, mind, and spirit. The Greeks believed that the three were interwoven, that all three needed to be on the same page when it came to healing as well as when it came to wellness. Interestingly enough, here we are thousands of years later and we are just now coming to that conclusion, we are just now realizing the wisdom of those ancient Greeks.

A look at the shelves of our bookstores attest to that. Whether it be the works of Dr. Deepak Chopra or Dr. Bernie Siegel or Dr. Norman Cousins or Joan Boryszenko, one reads of case after case in which the root cause of the illness lies within a conflict between the body, mind, and spirit. They've even spawned a new branch of medicine called psychoimmunology which sees the resolution of that conflict as one of the key ingredients for healing.

In a book called *Sound Mind, Sound Body*,[1] Dr. Ken Pellitere reviewed the lifestyles of some of the most successful, the most vibrant, the most dynamic, the most healthy individuals in the world today. In each and every case, it was quite clear that the heart, the mind, the body, and the soul were all on the same page. The individuals in question were running their lives with all those cylinders moving in unison, propelling them in a positive direction and being nurtured and cultivated along the way.

So whether it be illness or wellness, the key ingredients are the same. The mind, the body, and the soul all play a crucial part. You find that to be true as well when it comes to what someone is able to achieve and accomplish.

There has recently been a great deal of controversy surrounding IQ tests. A certain professor in a book called *The Bell Curve*[2] has stirred up a hornets' nest. As it turns out, the whole book is nonsense because the reality is that one can never comprise a test that measures intelligence. Furthermore, even if it could be done, it wouldn't mean anything because it would only measure one part of the person and not the whole person.

Time and time again, we've seen very intelligent people amount to nothing when it comes to life. We've seen people, whose brain knowledge far surpasses their peers', failing to achieve any of their goals for life. Intelligence means very little if along with it one doesn't also have enthusiasm, drive, emotion, desire, integrity, and honor. What holds true for illness and wellness holds true for success as well. Mind, heart, body, and soul must be nurtured, groomed, and harnessed for success ever to be possible. If any of those integral parts of the self are not on the same page, chances are strong that one will never accomplish what one sets out to achieve.

The expression "missing the mark by eighteen inches" is used in the business world. It's the reason given for why many people with great leadership potential and great talent never realize their potential. Eighteen inches is the distance between the head and the heart. All too often you find people saying the right things, knowing the right answers, and having all kinds of ability, but their hearts are not in it, and that makes all the difference in the world.

When I coached baseball, I always said that I wished I could do heart transfers because I coached many players who had all the physical tools necessary to be magnificent pitchers, catchers, or shortstops but didn't have the enthusiasm or the desire or the spirit to make it happen. On the other hand, I coached many a player who was all heart but who had very little physical ability. More often than not, he would start ahead of his more physically endowed counterparts. On more than one occasion I couldn't help but think how things could be different if I transferred the hearts. Boy, what a team I would have had! I would have had major league prospects on my roster.

Whether it be intelligence, physical ability, talent, or whatever, it all means nothing if there isn't the integration of body with mind, if there isn't the closing of the eighteen-inch gap between the head and the heart. And that goes as well when another important component is left out of the integration. There have been many people who have closed that eighteen-inch gap, who have done a good job combining their physical ability, their intelligence, and their heart; but they forgot to include the soul, and that's the most important piece of all.

An important meeting took place in 1923 at the Edgewater Beach Hotel in Chicago. It involved a group of business tycoons. Together these men controlled unfathomable sums of wealth and for years the media had trumpeted their success stories. On that day in Chicago, they assembled to enjoy their mutual success. What made the meeting memorable was what happened in the years that followed.

Samuel Insel, who was the president of the largest electric utility company in the United States, went on to become a fugitive from justice and he died literally in exile in a foreign country. Howard Hopsen, president of the largest gas company in the United States, would eventually find himself in the care of psychiatrists who committed him to an asylum for the remaining years of his life. Leon Fraser, president of one of the world's largest banks, went on to commit suicide. Albert Fall, who in 1923 was Secretary of the Interior to President Harding, would end up in jail many years later and be granted a pardon so he could die at home. I could go on with a list of the others at that meeting, but their stories are the same. All of these successful people closed the eighteen-inch gap between the head and the heart. They employed body, mind, and spirit in the pursuit of their goals. But they had no scruples; they were ruthless. They never took into account justice or integrity or fairness or compassion. Their families were left on the sidelines as they pursued their goals. They had it all together but they left out the soul and in the end they paid the price.

When Jesus was questioned in today's Gospel as to what was the most important commandment, the most important rule for life, he began by proposing that we love God with all the parts of the self. We must love God, not only with our minds, not only with our hearts, but with all of our minds and all of our hearts and all of our souls and all of our strength. He knew that if we integrated all those aspects of ourselves in our love for God, we would more than likely do the same for our love for life. By having all the parts of ourselves on the same page, we would realize health, we would realize success, we would realize fulfillment, we would realize inner peace. If any of those parts was disconnected from the whole, we probably would not realize any of it.

The next time you are out driving and your mind wanders and you make the wrong turn, be grateful that you didn't have an accident. Let it serve as an example of the importance of keeping body and mind on the same page, and not just body and mind, but soul and heart as well. Let it serve to inspire you to close any eighteen-inch gap that might be hurting your life.

---

1. Dr. Kenneth R. Pelletier, *Sound Mind, Sound Body* (New York: Simon & Schuster, 1994).

2. Richard J. Herrnstein and Charles Murray, *The Bell Curve* (New York: Free Press, 1994).

The Heroism Of Going On

Scripture Lesson: 2 Maccabees 7:1-2, 9-14
*... After he too had died, they maltreated
and tortured the fourth brother ...*

An attempt to address the concern over the lack of heroes in today's
society.

Recently a lot of television sets in the hospital were tuned to
the Turner Broadcasting Station. It might have been that the patients
were tired of the election reporting or the infomercials that were
on the other channels, but the greater reason was that movies starring
John Wayne were the featured attraction. The Turner Broadcasting
people were calling it "The Duke Week" and viewers were treated
to the various westerns for which Duke Wayne was famous.

It's interesting to see the continual popularity of John Wayne-
type movies. For many of us there is a fascination with the tough
guy, rugged individual character which he so often portrayed. We
love those old-time westerns and we like the contemporary imitations as well. Arnold Schwarzenegger and Steven Seagal are two
of Hollywood's biggest stars. Their movies, for the most part, are
of a John Wayne style. We love characters that demonstrate a real
toughness, who seem to epitomize real bravery, who seem to thrive
on tackling assignments and going into situations where most of
us would fear to tread. It might be because they portray a virtue
that seems for many of us to be vanishing today — courage.

It is unfortunate that we link courage with the rugged individual,
tough guy character because their brand of courage is hardly a good
representation of the virtue. Courage today seems hard to find, but
perhaps the reason lies in the fact that we look for it in all the
wrong places. We long for it in a form that seldom does it justice.

In that wonderful Harper Lee novel *To Kill a Mockingbird,*[1]
Atticus Finch, a country lawyer in a small Alabama town, sent his
son Jem to read every afternoon to a neighbor lady, Mrs. Dubose,

who was dying of cancer. He tried to teach his son that, despite her racial prejudice, she was a remarkable woman. She was on daily doses of morphine, needing it to kill her pain. But when her doctor told her that she had only a few weeks to live, she decided to stop the morphine, enduring the pain, so that she would be "beholden to nothing and nobody" when she died.

On the evening of the day she died, Atticus explains to Jem why he had sent him to read to her.

> *"I wanted you to see something about her," said Atticus. "I wanted you to see what real courage is, instead of getting the idea that courage is a man with a gun in his hand. It's when you're licked before you begin, but you begin anyway and you see it through no matter what, that's what real courage is! It's when you're in pain, when you're suffering, and you go on, that's what real courage is! According to her views, Mrs. Dubose died 'beholden to nothing and nobody.' She was the bravest person I ever knew."*

It seems that so often when we reference bravery and courage, we look at the heroes of war, the athlete who plays despite pain, explorers who tread into unknown territory, the statesman who rallied people and helped topple a corrupt regime, the John Wayne type who enters a lion's den with hardly an ounce of fear. One shouldn't diminish or demean any of those samples of courage. We wouldn't be where we are today without the Admiral Stocksdales, the Lech Walesas, and the Lewis and Clarks. We are inspired by the play of Bernie Kosar who stayed in the football game despite a broken ankle. We appreciate a person who boldly challenges something or someone which others haven't the guts to do.

But for the most part, those exhibitions of courage have received their rewards. Those exhibitions of courage are hailed and acknowledged. Those exhibitions of courage have enjoyed strong support and high esteem. The courage to which Atticus Finch alluded has none of that. The courage he described is the type often overlooked. It is the kind often missed. It's the courage that goes unrecognized, yet it speaks volumes for strength and for valor and

130

for nobility and for gallantry. It is of a caliber that often pales the more popular and more external versions of courage.

Allister Maclean, not the famous novelist but the famous preacher, tells of an incident in the Scottish Highlands. A little group of young people were talking about heroism, saying that everybody had sooner or later to practice some kind of heroism. A young man turned to an old woman who looked very ordinary and very serene. He did not know that life had been very cruel to her, that she had sustained and endured countless tragedies. He figured that nothing great could be found in a life that was so ordinary and so plain as hers. Just to be smart, he asked her, "What kind of heroism do you practice?" She looked at the young man with her piercing eyes and her rugged face and she replied, "I practice the heroism of going on!"

The greatest examples of courage, the most moving portrayals of bravery, are most often found among simple and ordinary people who somehow manage to keep on living, who somehow manage to move ahead with their lives despite the misery and the tragedy and the poverty that surrounds them. Instead of resigning themselves to resentment and misery, they accept life as it is and heroically go on.

Samuel Johnson was an eighteenth century literary genius. Like many who contributed things of lasting value to history, his personal life was filled with tragedy. His was a life of loneliness and melancholy. From his boyhood as a half-blind and half-deaf awkward youth, to his old age when he suffered from dropsy and bronchitis and lung disease, and all but abandoned by his wife and family, Johnson managed to keep a semblance of dignity pursuing a literary career despite all the excuses to quit.

Johnson was never cited for his courage. He was not recognized as a literary genius in his day. It was only long after his death that such things would come to light. In the world in which he lived, Johnson was seen as a simple and serene and ordinary individual much like that woman in the Allister Maclean incident. Not too many noticed nor knew that he practiced the heroism of going on.

The same can be said for many others whom history has recorded as major contributors of things of lasting value. Vincent van Gogh sold only one painting in his career and was dependent upon the generous but limited support of his brother. He would often not eat for days just so he could afford to buy painting materials. Johann Sebastian Bach was panned by the critics of his day. The only decent commission he ever received was from a composition of some relaxing pieces of music for a Russian envoy. He had a family of eight children and had to struggle hard to feed them. Mozart was so poor that all his life was a heartbreaking battle with poverty. He was buried in a pauper's grave. John Keats was so crippled by poverty that it is an agony to read about his life.

Van Gogh, Mozart, Bach, and Keats never brandished any weapons. They didn't rally forces against an unjust cause. They didn't venture into unexplored territory. They weren't cited or hailed in their lifetimes. They entered no lion's den. Their courage however goes beyond question. They struggled against immeasurable difficulties. They survived the most destitute of life's conditions. They pursued the development of their talents despite the multiple forces working against them. They were simple and ordinary people practicing the heroism of going on.

Iif one has a hard time locating examples of courage, if one is complaining about the lack of heroes in modern life, if one is distressed because courage is seen as a vanishing virtue, perhaps one should begin talking to some of the simple and ordinary people around them who aren't so lucky. Perhaps one should talk to those whose lives are filled with pain and suffering and tragedy. Courage and heroism do abound in the world around us, but it is not centered on nerve and muscle. It is centered on the human spirit surviving against the most difficult and painful of life's circumstances.

My work at the hospital awakens me often to that truth. There are people here on a regular basis for chemotherapy, and many of them go through hell. There are people who have surgery that leaves them with a permanent trache in their throats which has to be cleaned several times a day. There are people who have strokes and they can't talk and they can't walk and now they face endless hours of therapy. There are parents whose newborn child has multiple handicaps. There are families who come here each day to sit with their loved one whose Alzheimer's disease has turned him or her into a stranger who now has no recollection of his/her existence. All of those people, all of those families, are practitioners of the heroism of going on. They show tremendous courage, and their demonstration of courage far exceeds anything you'll ever find in a John Wayne movie. They are the bravest people I know.

The issue of courage jumps out at us in today's first reading. It's the recounting of the story of the heroism of seven brothers and their mother. Rather than violate God's law, they willingly suffered torture and death and they did so, not all at once, but one by one, with the rest of the family standing by. Their courage rested not just in the endurance of their own pain and suffering, but also in the endurance of watching the pain and suffering of the people they loved.

Unfortunately, that twofold display of courage is not unusual. There have been other families in sacred scripture who endured a similar tragedy. The history of the church is filled with tens of thousands of heroic and courageous people who gave their lives so that the message of God could be heard. Today we may not see that much heroism and courage, but maybe it is because we've come to associate it only with the shedding of blood. Maybe it is because we've come to identify it only with acts of outward bravery. But who is to say that courage and heroism for God's causes aren't being demonstrated in different ways?

There is much courage and there is much heroism going on today. It doesn't get the fanfare. It doesn't get the press. It's not easily recognized. But it's there in the poor, the sick, the lame and the blind. It's there in the Mrs. Duboses and the Samuel Johnsons and the Vincent van Goghs and the John Keats, and even in the people right here in this place of worship. It's there in those who, when found with great trial and great suffering, manage to go on, and in doing so they are not just practicing heroism, but they're also giving witness to the spirit of God alive in our world.

In Japan the bamboo tree is a symbol of prosperity. The pine tree is a symbol of longevity. And the plum tree is a symbol of courage. The plum tree seems out of place as a symbol for courage. One might expect an old stately tree with sturdy roots and worn bark. The plum tree was chosen because the plum tree blooms very early in spring when there is still snow on the ground.

Courage, you see, is not marked simply by what we do but by when and where we do it. True courage can be found in the one who stands firm and flowers even in the face of difficulties and opposition, even in the face of the snowstorms of life.

The next time you want to see examples of courage, don't go to a movie theater. Go to a hospital or a nursing home or a Blind Association meeting or some rehab center or some broken-down apartment of some fledgling artist. They are usually the places where plum trees abound.

---

1. Harper Lee, *To Kill a Mockingbird* (Philadelphia: Lippincott Press, 1960).

Maalox Moments

Scripture Lesson: John 14:23-29
... do not let your hearts be troubled ...

Unfortunately, Maalox moments seem to outnumber peaceful moments. I offer a few reasons why.

The makers of Maalox have come up with a series of commercials that have highlighted situations which, in their estimation, are tailor-made for the use of their product. In one of those commercials, one is taken into a home with kids running about screaming, the dog knocking over a vase, the bathtub spilling water onto the floor. The toast is smoking in the toaster. The doorbell is ringing and the telephone is clanging. The camera then zeroes in on the haggard look of the mother who, at this point, could easily qualify for a nerve transplant. It's then that one hears the announcement: "It's another one of those Maalox moments."

Maalox, of course, is for upset stomachs and there are few among us who have not had their stomachs upset by the stress and the worry and the anxiety common to life. Maalox moments occur all too frequently. Rare is the life that hasn't had a large share of those moments.

We live in an age when anxiety is at an all-time high, when tensions are mounting to increasingly steep levels, when stress and worry are often the order of the day. A glance at pharmaceutical statistics proves the point. Valium is the most prescribed drug in America today. Close behind is Tagamet, and that's used to treat ulcers which are often the result of worry carried too far. Of the top-selling over-the-counter drugs, Maalox and Excedrin and Rolaids are near the top of the list. Their distinct role is to treat the physical effects that have come to us compliments of stress, worry, and anxiety.

It seems apparent that the words of Jesus in our Gospel today haven't been taken very seriously by very many people. Jesus tells

135

his disciples, and, in essence, tells us, "I leave behind with you peace. I give you my own peace. You must not be distressed or fearful." You have to understand that Jesus' use of the word peace in this passage is very unique. It was common in the days in which he lived for people to greet each other with the word peace. But Jesus isn't using the word peace as a greeting, he's using it in terms of a bequest. Jesus says, "I'm giving you peace," and he fully expects that the peace will reign supreme in the hearts and minds of all his followers.

That being so, why is it that so few of us realize that peace? Why is it that our lives are filled much more with Maalox moments than they are with peaceful moments? Maybe one of the reasons lies in the fact that all too often we get worked up over things which we can't do anything about.

There is a legend about a burdened old man who, along his tiresome way, met an angel. The old man was bent under the enormous weight of a great burlap sack across his shoulders and on his back. It was so heavy it was a wonder he could walk. The angel said, "What is it you have in the sack?" The man replied, "In there are my worries!" The angel said, "Empty them out, let me see them." With great effort, the old man lowered the huge sack from his back and turned out the contents. Out first came yesterday, and then tomorrow. And the angel picked up yesterday and threw it aside and said, "You don't need that because yesterday is in the hands of God and no amount of worrying will change it." Then the angel picked up tomorrow and said "You don't need this because tomorrow is in the hands of God and no amount of worrying will change it." In the end, the old man had no worries to put in the sack.

It's so often the case that much of what we worry about lies beyond our control. Maalox moments are often the result of things we can do nothing about.

Members of Alcoholics Anonymous pray a great prayer that all of us should think about adopting. It's called the serenity prayer. It reads: "God grant me the serenity to accept the things I cannot change, the courage to change the things I can, and the wisdom to know the difference." Of all the phrases by which people live their lives, I can think of none that contains more good sense than that. Within it is the notion that there are things that happen to us in life that despite how much we would wish them different, they will not be different. We, if we are to survive, must accept those things as they are, doing so with grace and with dignity.

Walter Underwood, in his book *Being Hopeful, Being Human,*[1] talks of a man who developed a worry table. He wrote down all the things he was worried about and then classified them. He quickly discovered that forty percent of the time he was worried about things that would probably never happen; thirty percent of the time he stewed about decisions he had already made; twelve percent of the time he fretted about becoming ill; ten percent of the time he was troubled about his friends and their children; and eight percent of the time he was worried about immediate problems that he needed to solve. After reviewing his worry table, it became obvious that he could discard 92 percent of his worries.

That's not a bad exercise for us to adopt. Perhaps in constructing our own worry table, we'd find that one of the reasons why we have more Maalox moments than peaceful moments might be that we worry too much about things which will either never happen or which we can do nothing about.

Then there is the matter of getting all nerved up because of things we lack, failing to realize and appreciate all the things we have.

When a colleague came by yesterday, he asked me what I'd be preaching on this Sunday. I told him that I'd be talking about worries. He then proceeded to present to me the following syllogism: There are only two things to worry about in life, and that's being healthy or being sick. If you're healthy, you have nothing to worry about. If you're sick, you have two things to worry about, getting better or getting worse. If you're getting better, you have nothing to worry about. If you're getting worse, you have two things to worry about, surviving or dying. If you survive, you have nothing to worry about. If you die, you have two things to worry about, going to heaven or going to hell. If you're going to heaven, you have nothing to worry about. If you go to hell, you'll be so busy shaking hands with your friends that you won't have any time to worry.

Sometimes what it takes to go from a Maalox moment to a peaceful moment comes down to a matter of keeping things in perspective.

There is an interesting story about J.C. Penney,[2] the tycoon who founded the large chain of stores that bear his name. He suffered tremendous financial losses during the Depression. He worried about them to such an extent that he had a nervous breakdown and was confined to a sanitarium for months. The doctors worked with him but to no avail. He became increasingly worse until one night he decided he was near death and so he wrote farewell notes to each of his loved ones. The next morning, to his great surprise, he was still breathing. He hadn't died. As he contemplated his fate, he heard a number of voices singing a tune that sounded vaguely familiar to him. Struggling out of bed, he walked down the corridor to the chapel, the source of the voices. As he opened the door, he heard the words that were being sung:

> *Be not dismayed what'er betide,*
> *God will take care of you.*
> *Beneath his wings of love abide,*
> *God will take care of you.*

Mr. Penney remembered that song from his childhood. It evoked within him an overwhelming sense of the care, the kindness, and the love of Almighty God. He suddenly began to image his blessings instead of his worries. He began to take note of the fact that there were a lot of things right in his life, that he had a lot of things going for him which many people didn't have. He was blessed by family, friends, and business associates who never left his side. God had indeed taken care of him and blessed him but he was too filled with worry to take notice. J.C. Penney began to get well quickly and he went on to live to the ripe old age of 92. He never forgot the old song that enabled him to image his blessings instead of his worries, to image all he had instead of all he lost.

So it goes with many of us. We worry about getting ahead. We worry about accomplishing something. We worry about paying off a debt. We worry about meeting a deadline. They are legitimate and important worries. But we fail, in the meantime, to appreciate and relish the immense amount of blessings we still have and which will still be there regardless of how successful or unsuccessful we are with our ventures.

Another reason why our Maalox moments might outnumber our peaceful moments could stem from the fact that we have unrealistic expectations about life.

S.I. Hayakawa, the former Senator from California, once wrote a very telling piece[3] about bus drivers from Chicago. When he was young, he used to ride the bus down Indiana Avenue, a street that was often blocked by badly parked cars and tractor trailers backing into warehouses and maneuvering in every which way. While he rode the bus, he observed two types of bus drivers. One type seemed to expect to be able to ride down Indiana Avenue without interruption. Every time things got blocked, they would get steamed up with rage. They would blow their horns, and they would lean out of the bus to yell at the drivers of the tractor trailers. At the end of the day one can reasonably assume that they were nervous wrecks. When they went home, they were probably jittery and hypersensitive, menaces to their wives and children.

The other type of bus driver, Hayakawa observed, drove their buses fully expecting Indiana Avenue to be blocked, a realistic expectation because it usually was. They would sit and wait for minutes at a time without fretting. They would be whistling a tune or they would be writing their reports or they would be glancing at a magazine that they brought along for just such stoppages. Hayakawa concluded his essay by remarking how in confronting the same objective situation some bus drivers lived a hellish life of nervous tension while other bus drivers had a nice relaxing job with plenty of time to rest.

Many of our Maalox moments stem from the fact that we expect life to be perfect, free from flaws, interruptions, mistakes, and turmoil. Let's face it! It never is! The better we learn to cope with life's inevitable shortcomings, the better will be our nerves, the less stressful will be our lives.

Another reason why we may not be realizing Christ's bequest of peace could stem from the fact that we've centered too much of our lives upon ourselves. We end up having nothing else to think about except our aches, our pains, our worries.

The Healing Power of Doing Good[4] is a book packed with testimony about the immense benefits which come our way when we give of ourselves for the sake of another. One statistic noted that sixty percent of the people who volunteered themselves for something realized as a result a decrease in feelings of helplessness, despair, and anxiety. One senior citizen started doing volunteer work at both her winter residence in Florida and her summer home in Minnesota. She volunteered her services tutoring young children in math. According to her, volunteering was the best thing she could have done for herself. Working with children not only made her feel good, but it also got her to forget the aches, the pains, and the bits of arthritis that worried and troubled her. When our life centers around ourselves, we have a lot of time on our hands and when that is so, our minds have nothing else to do but manufacture worries.

There are many reasons why our Maalox moments outnumber our peaceful moments. These are indeed stressful times. Anxiety and tension are indeed on the rise. That's all the more reason to take Jesus up on his Gospel offer. Jesus has left behind a bequest of peace. It's time we collected our inheritance.

---

1. Walter L. Underwood, *Being Human, Being Hopeful* (Nashville: Abingdon Press, 1987), p. 12.

2. *Ibid.*, p. 16.

3. S.I. Hayakawa, *Symbols, Status, and Personality* (New York: Harcourt Brace Jovanovich, 1963), p. 81.

4. Allen Luks with Peggy Payne, *The Healing Power of Doing Good* (New York: Ballantine Books, 1991).

What To Do About The Loss Of Someone Precious

Scripture Lesson: Psalm 23
> *... though I walk through the darkest valley ...*

An effort to console families who frequent our chapel for a memorial service commemorating those who have died in the hospital.

A mother sends her child on an errand, and it takes a long time for him to get home. When he finally comes back, his mother says, "Where were you? We were worried about you!" And the boy said, "There was a kid down the street and his tricycle broke and he was crying because he couldn't fix it. I felt bad for him so I tried to help." And his mother said to him, "Are you trying to tell me that you know how to fix tricycles?" "Of course not," said the boy, "I sat down and helped him cry."

We've come here together tonight to help each other cry, to stand by one another with our broken hearts.

It's very hard to attend memorial services. They have a way of repuncturing wounds, reopening sores, and bringing home the point that you're never really going to get over that awful loss of that one who was so precious. But I think the tears, the wounds and the sores are all tributes to that person. They are living reminders of how special and how beautiful was that life that has been taken away.

But it can't stop there. A greater tribute is paid to those people we loved if we reflect in our lives the lessons on life they taught us. I can't think of a better memorial for someone who died than lives lived more fully and more beautifully thanks to the impact of that life now gone.

The late Rabbi Sam Porrath once said that those who have left us would like nothing more than to be granted a curtain call, another chance to appear on the stage of life. We grant them that chance, that curtain call, by displaying through our lives the positive qualities and the beautiful characteristics that were the trademarks of those we love.

When the Royal Palace in Tehran, Iran, was being built the architect sent an order for mirrors to cover the entrance walls. Just as the palace was about to be completed, the mirrors finally arrived in huge crates. The workers took the crates apart and, to their dismay, all they found were broken pieces of mirrors. They were all smashed in transit. The architect, as you might imagine, was depressed. The final part of the construction would now have to come to a halt until a new shipment of mirrors arrived. The whole construction crew was at a standstill until the architect came up with a brilliant idea. He took the broken pieces of mirror and began to fit them onto the entrance wall, one piece at a time, as though he were constructing a mosaic. The end result was an entranceway that would take your breath away. The entranceway looks as though it's covered with diamonds. The broken pieces of mirror produce a crystal effect, throwing out the colors of the rainbow to all who pass them by.

Your hearts have been broken, your lives have been shattered by the death of your loved one. But if you can pick up the pieces, if you can gather up the broken parts of your heart and from them construct a new and beautiful life, just think what you are telling the world about your loved one. You are letting everyone know that he or she was a special person, because look at what a positive impact that person made upon the lives of those left behind.

We are here tonight to honor someone loved very dearly. We honor that someone through tears, through readings, through music, through slides, through the tolling of names. But we honor them even more by incorporating the exceptional qualities of their lives into the fabric and texture of our own lives, thus providing them with a curtain call. We allow their lives, their beauty, their specialness to live on through us, displaying from the broken pieces of our shattered lives a wonderful mosaic throwing out rainbows to all who come near.

An Oscar was given for the song "The Wind Beneath My Wings" from the movie *Beaches*. It was a movie about two women whose early childhood friendship blossomed and grew to the extent that you couldn't help but be emotionally moved when an early death ends the friendship. The Oscar-winning song, sung by Bette Midler, was a testimony to that extraordinary friendship. She refers to the fact that she can fly higher than an eagle because of the wind of love that came from her special friend.

The relationship you had with your deceased loved one, no matter how brief or how long it may have been, was a relationship that meant the world to you. Pay tribute to it by allowing the wind of that love to propel you to fly higher than eagles, to propel you to make something beautiful out of the fragments of your broken heart. What a wonderful way of giving your loved one a curtain call. What a wonderful way of giving testimony to the wonderful gift God gave you in the person of that loved one now enjoying eternal life.